INTRODUCING CHINA

INTRODUCING CHINA

THE WORLD'S OLDEST GREAT POWER CHARTS ITS NEXT COMEBACK

RON HUISKEN

THE AUSTRALIAN NATIONAL UNIVERSITY

E PRESS

ANU

E PRESS

Published by ANU E Press
The Australian National University
Canberra ACT 0200, Australia
Email: anuepress@anu.edu.au
This title is also available online at: http://epress.anu.edu.au/introducing_china_citation.html

National Library of Australia
Cataloguing-in-Publication entry

Author:	Huisken, Ron
Title:	Introducing China : the world's oldest great power charts its next comeback / Ron Huisken.
ISBN:	9781921666186 (pbk) 9781921666193 (pdf)
Series:	Canberra papers on strategy and defence ; 176
Notes:	Bibliography.
Subjects:	China--Politics and government--21st century. China--Economic conditions--21st century. China--Foreign relations.
Dewey Number:	327.51

The *Canberra Papers on Strategy and Defence* series is a collection of publications arising principally from research undertaken at the SDSC. Canberra Papers have been peer reviewed since 2006. All Canberra Papers are available for sale: visit the SDSC website at <http://rspas.anu.edu.au/sdsc/canberra_papers.php> for abstracts and prices. Electronic copies (in pdf format) of most SDSC Working Papers published since 2002 may be downloaded for free from the SDSC website at <http://rspas.anu.edu.au/sdsc/working_papers.php>. The entire Working Papers series is also available on a 'print on demand' basis.

Strategic and Defence Studies Centre Publications Program Advisory Review Panel: Emeritus Professor Paul Dibb; Professor Desmond Ball; Professor David Horner; Professor Hugh White; Professor William Tow; Professor Anthony Milner; Professor Virginia Hooker; Dr Coral Bell; Dr Pauline Kerr.

Strategic and Defence Studies Centre Publications Program Editorial Board: Professor Hugh White; Dr Brendan Taylor; Dr Christian Enemark.

Cover design by ANU E Press

Contents

About the Author

Ron Huisken joined the Strategic and Defence Studies Centre at the Australian National University in 2001, after nearly twenty years working in the Australian government departments of Foreign Affairs and Trade, Defence, and Prime Minister and Cabinet. His research interests include US security policies, multilateral security processes in East Asia, alliance management and non-proliferation. Dr Huisken has authored numerous works, including a number of working and Canberra papers published by the Strategic and Defence Studies Centre. This paper represents the author's views alone. It has been drawn entirely from open sources, and has no official status or endorsement.

Acknowledgements

A number of colleagues offered valuable comments on all or parts of the manuscript at various stages, notably Richard Brabin-Smith, Stephan Frühling, Paul Dibb and Chris Barrie. The author also wishes to acknowledge Meredith Thatcher who edited the manuscript with her customary flair and commitment. Responsibility for the remaining shortcomings of the manuscript naturally rests with the author.

Acronyms and Abbreviations

ACDA	Arms Control and Disarmament Agency
APT	ASEAN Plus Three
ARF	ASEAN Regional Forum
ASEAN	Association of Southeast Asian Nations
CCP	Chinese Communist Party
CPI	Consumer Price Index
DIA	Defense Intelligence Agency
DMZ	demilitarised zone
GDP	Gross Domestic Product
GNP	Gross National Product
IAEA	International Atomic Energy Agency
ICBM	intercontintental ballistic missile
IISS	International Institute for Strategic Studies
MFN	Most Favoured Nation
NATO	North Atlantic Treaty Organization
NPT	Non-Proliferation Treaty
OECD	Organisation for Economic Co-operation and Development
PLA	People's Liberation Army
PPP	purchasing power parity
PRC	People's Republic of China
QDR	Quadrennial Defense Review
R&D	research and development
SCO	Shanghai Cooperation Organisation
SIOP	Single Integrated Operational Plan
SIPRI	Stockholm International Peace Research Institute
SLBM	submarine-launched ballistic missile
SSBN	Ship Submersible Ballistic Nuclear
UNSC	United Nations Security Council
WMD	Weapons of Mass Destruction
WTO	World Trade Organization

Preface

The preparation of this monograph was made possible by an Australian Research Council Linkage Grant under which the ARC matched initial funding from the Department of Defence. The author and the Strategic and Defence Studies Centre are grateful to both organisations for this support. The monograph was developed primarily to support students in the Graduate Studies in Strategy and Defence (GSSD) Masters program. It is hoped, of course, that it will also be of interest to undergraduate and post-graduate students in other fields such as international relations and political science, given the growing importance of China in these disciplines.

Introduction

China intrigues in so many ways: a mesmerisingly large population, an intimidatingly long political and cultural tradition, a reputation for looking at and thinking about issues in very distinctive ways, a cultural predisposition to communicate in indirect and ambiguous ways, a continuous tradition of authoritarian and opaque governance, and so forth. Until about fifteen years ago, however, China was an interest for a small band of specialists. That has all changed. China is now a compulsory object of understanding and analysis for all students of strategy, international relations and global economics.

We know that China has dominated East Asia in the past. Indeed, unlike every other major power in today's world, China's fortunes have surged and ebbed *several* times over the last two millennia, with both peaks and troughs often enduring for centuries. It might even be said that, in the more distant past, China loomed so large in the affairs of East Asia that it dominated the region both when it was strong and when it was weak. With China now widely regarded as dependably resurgent and destined again to become a major force in shaping the destiny of East Asia and the wider world, some contend that this will represent its fourth re-emergence as one of the first-rank nations in the world.[1]

The Chinese make little secret of the fact that their natural reference point in this regard is not the likes of Japan, Germany, France or the United Kingdom but the titan of the contemporary world, the United States of America. The United States has been an integral part of China's saga for well over a century. This is hardly surprising as this is the timeframe in which the United States emerged, first, as the largest single economy in the world and then, progressively, as the dominant comprehensive global power. What is certainly of interest, however, is the variety of roles it has played in respect of China. The United States was a prominent member of the group of industrialised states that broke down imperial China's resistance to open trade and investment—an often harshly imposed transformation that the Chinese remember as the 'century of humiliation' (roughly 1850–1950). The United States was also a *mediator* between Japan and Russia following their war in 1904–1905. The settlement included recognising Russian territorial claims in northern Manchuria and that Korea was a Japanese protectorate—both issues of profound interest and concern to imperial China. Since then the United States has been China's *saviour*, in crushing Japan in 1945; China's primary *enemy* from the time their forces clashed in Korea in 1950, although the United States was ultimately pushed into second place by

---

1   Wang Gungwu, 'The Fourth Rise of China: Cultural Implications', *China: An International Journal*, vol. 2, September 2004, pp. 311–22.

the Soviet Union; China's *informal protector*, from the time of US-China re-engagement in 1972 until the demise of the Soviet Union in 1989–91; and China's *economic partner* since China's embrace of the market economy in 1978 (most analysts would agree that, taking markets, capital and technology together, the United States has been the most important external factor in China's economic miracle over the past thirty years). US Secretary of State Hillary Clinton echoed an almost universal sentiment to the effect that the US-China relationship will be the most important bilateral relationship in the world in the twenty-first century.[2] This, of course, is tantamount to acknowledging that China, and only China, is securely on track to becoming a *peer competitor* of the United States.

In terms of hard numbers, China has a long way to go before it will step into the arena currently monopolised by the United States. But, in terms of perceptions and expectations, China has certainly achieved Mao Zedong's declaration in 1949 that China would once again 'stand up' in the community of states.

Table 1: Shares of World GDP, 1000–1998 (per cent)

	1000	1500	1820	1870	1913	1950	1973	1998
Western Europe	8.7	17.9	23.6	33.6	33.5	26.3	25.7	20.6
Western Offshoots	0.7	0.5	1.9	10.2	21.7	30.6	25.3	25.1
Japan	2.7	3.1	3.0	2.3	2.6	3.0	7.7	7.7
Asia (excluding Japan)	67.6	62.1	56.2	36.0	21.9	15.5	16.4	29.5
Latin America	3.9	2.9	2.0	2.5	4.5	7.9	8.7	8.7
Eastern Europe and former USSR	4.6	5.9	8.8	11.7	13.1	13.1	12.9	5.3
Africa	11.8	7.4	4.5	3.7	2.7	3.6	3.3	3.1
World	100.0	100.0	100.0	100.0	100.0	100.0	100.0	100.0

(*Source*: Angus Maddison, *The World Economy: A Millennial Perspective*, OECD, Paris, 2001, p. 127)

The last era in which China was strong and dominant in its region ended more than two hundred years ago. This can be seen in the Organisation for Economic Co-operation and Development (OECD) estimates of world Gross Domestic Product (GDP) extending back to the year 1000 (although with greater confidence naturally attached to the estimates for more recent times). The share of world output attributed to Asia without Japan—a figure dominated by China and, to a lesser extent, India—fell precipitously between 1820 and 1950, and remained low into the 1970s. The figure of 15-16 per cent of world output in 1950–70, compared to more than 50 per cent 150 years earlier, suggests strongly that standards of well-being in China fell in absolute as well as relative terms. Small wonder that modern, Communist China labelled this era 'the period of

---

2   Hillary Rodham Clinton, 'Clinton: Security and Opportunity for the Twenty-first Century', *Foreign Affairs*, vol. 86, no. 6, November/December 2007, pp. 2–18, available at <http://www.foreignaffairs. org/20071101faessay86601/hillary-rodham-clinton/security-and-opportunity-for-the-twenty-first-century. html>, accessed 24 June 2009. Article written when Clinton was a US Presidential candidate.

humiliation', and as a set of circumstances that epitomised the dangers of being politically and militarily weak *and* open economically (the latter quality having been essentially imposed by the industrialised West).

The period since China's last heyday under the Ming and early Qing dynasties—a period of about two centuries—is well beyond the timeframe that allows easy inferences to be drawn about today and tomorrow. There can be no doubt that China's past contains important clues to its future: the art lies in discriminating between what has truly become history and what is likely to be of enduring importance.

With China now heading for a further re-incarnation as a heavyweight on the international scene, the questions attracting everyone's interest include: How strong and coherent and focused could China become? Where will China focus its strength and influence? What instruments of power and influence will China give preference to? Are perceptions of past glories and embarrassments (and beliefs about how these fluctuating fortunes came about) important in shaping the thinking of China's elite in the twenty-first century? Do the Chinese know where they want to go and what they will do when they get there, or will it be more a case of figuring it out as they go along and making the most of whatever circumstances they find themselves in? Is it important that China retains an authoritarian government, and will this be an enduring characteristic of its present revival?

The dimensions of China's economic performance since the 'reform and opening up' in 1978 are well known and will not be discussed in this paper. In 1963, despite having a population 3–4 times as large as the United States, China's Gross National Product (GNP), converted at estimated purchasing power parity rates rather than the official exchange rate, measured about 11 per cent that of the United States. Fifteen years later, in 1978, the differential had narrowed modestly to 18 per cent. At that time, China's GDP per capita was still just 4 per cent of the global average, about the same as it had been 20 years earlier, in 1960.[3] Over the next thirty years, China made up ground at a spectacular rate, sustaining an average real rate of growth of GDP of nearly 10 per cent. By 2008, using official exchange rates, China was the third largest economy in the world, poised just below Japan, and certain to achieve the number two ranking, probably by 2009. Using purchasing power parity (PPP) rates, China's economy in 2008 was already number two in the world and, indeed, some 80 per cent larger than that of Japan.[4]

---

3   See Charles van Marrewijk, *International Trade and the World Economy,* Oxford University Press, Oxford, February 2002.
4   These GDP comparisons are based on estimates prepared by the Central Intelligence Agency and convert estimates of China's GDP into US dollars using both official and PPP rates. See *CIA World Factbook,* available at <https://www.cia.gov/library/publications/the-world-factbook/rankorder/2004rank.html>, accessed 24

Late in 2007, however, the World Bank published the results of a major undertaking to update PPP estimates for its member states: the new rate for China suggests that its GDP should be revised downward by a whopping 40 per cent. Clearly, these new figures do not mean that China's visible economic vibrancy has been to an important extent illusionary. What it does mean is that the penetration of economic development within China is substantially less than previously thought. As goods and services within China are more costly than previously thought, so the purchasing power of the Yuan is lower than previously thought. The World Bank now estimates that the PPP rate is closer to just twice as strong as the official exchange rate rather than four times as strong. It will take time for this new estimate to filter through the community of analysts that manipulate economic data. The most obvious consequence, clearly, is that the timeframe in which China is expected to become the largest economy in the world has slipped out well beyond 2020. But other calculations, including some estimates of China's military expenditure and of the share of GDP that China devotes to the military, will also be affected as new estimates are prepared and begin to be employed for analytical purposes.

Coping with the consequences of its stunning economic performance has and will present China with some difficult policy choices—especially in the fields of environment, water and energy security, and sharply increased income disparities between urban and rural communities. Few analysts, however, are prepared to argue that China's development is inherently fragile, that the political leadership will find one or more of these challenges to be insurmountable and that China's climb to the rank of one of the world's preeminent states will be seriously disrupted.

June 2009. The figures for 1963 and 1978 are also based on CIA estimates using PPP rates, but were taken from the relevant editions of *World Military Expenditure and Arms Transfers, US Arms Control and Disarmament Agency,* Washington, DC.

Chapter 1
Imperial China: Practice Makes Perfect?

The Yellow River in Northern China is one of four regions with a legitimate claim to being the 'cradle of civilisation'—the other three being the Nile in present-day Egypt; the Tigress/Euphrates in present-day Iraq; and the Indus in India/Pakistan[1] In each of these regions, evidence dating back beyond four thousand years has been found of people living in settled communities, growing and storing food, specializing in particular skills and exchanging goods and services among themselves.

Things moved pretty slowly in those days. In China, just three dynasties presided over the ensuing 1800 years: the Xia for over five centuries (approximately 2000–1450 BC); the Shang, for three centuries (1450–1122 BC); and the Zhou for nine centuries (1122–221 BC)—still the record). The later emperors of the Zhou presided over ethnic Chinese (or Han) communities that had expanded well north of the Yellow River and to south of the Yangzi River in central China, as well as eastward to the coast and westward along and between these two great rivers.

From around 500 BC, Zhou authority began to erode and conflict within the broader Chinese community escalated. Over time, the warring groups coalesced into seven larger polities that considered themselves separate entities that had their own army, collected their own taxes, concluded treaties and so forth.

Chinese expansion to the north and west led to contact with the nomadic tribes of these regions, known today as Manchuria and Mongolia. The determining commodity was the horse which the nomads traded for the grain, cloth, tools and utensils produced by the settled Chinese. This practice has been traced back to around 700 BC (although it undoubtedly extends back much further) and was to become a defining influence on the history of the Chinese people. For the next two thousand years, the nomadic craving for Chinese products remained strong. Chinese entanglement with the nomadic peoples to their north, northwest and to the west turned into an endless cycle of attempts to befriend, placate, deter, defeat, conquer, subjugate and Sinocise them. One or other combination of these stratagems often worked for long periods. Over the centuries, as China's

---

1   The broad outlines of the following, exceedingly short, account of imperial China is drawn primarily from three sources: Warren I. Cohen, *East Asia at the Center,* Columbia University Press, New York, 2000; Michael D. Swaine and Ashley J. Tellis, *Interpreting China's Grand Strategy: Past, Present, and Future*, Rand Corporation, Santa Monica, 2000, available at <http://rand.org/pubs/monograph_reports/MR1121/>, accessed 24 June 2009; and Ross Terrill, *The New Chinese Empire and What It Means for the United States,* Basic Books, New York, 2004.

fortunes waxed and waned, these stratagems had been revived, adapted and reapplied over and over again. With occasional, and significant, exceptions, China's imperial ambitions always addressed the same regions—the heartland of the nomadic tribes that would neither leave them alone nor quietly accept that they were considered inferior to the Chinese people and should coexist as subordinate neighbours: Manchuria, Mongolia, Xinjiang and Tibet. As it has several times in the past, today's China incorporates nearly all of these regions.

In previous centuries, there were three periods when China's power and influence underwent prolonged surges. On these occasions, dynamic leadership, internal cohesion, and national economic strength came together to allow offensive security policies, creative foreign policies, the flourishing of trade and the vigorous projection of Chinese culture and traditions. The dynasties associated with these rises to conspicuous and unambiguous pre-eminence are the Qin-Han from 221 BC, Sui-Tang from 581 AD and Ming-Qing from 1368 AD.

In each case, the extent of the territory over which China's emperor exercised direct control expanded very considerably. Also, in each case, China's surge to undisputed pre-eminence occurred in the first half of the dynastic period, with the latter periods characterised by ineffective leadership, internal instability and, in the case of the Han and Tang dynasties, imperial contraction. An anomaly that we will examine below is how the borders of modern China came to embrace even more extensive territories to the north and west than any other dynasty despite more than 150 years of precipitous decline between 1800 and 1949—that is, despite the Qing emperors proving embarrassingly ineffectual from around 1800 onwards, the disruptions of civil war in the 1920s and 1930s, invasion and partial occupation (by Japan) from 1937 to 1945 and then resumed civil war between 1945 and 1949.

China's first rise

As noted earlier, for the last three hundred years or so of its recorded reign, the authority of the Zhou emperors was nominal at best, as the component kingdoms of the Chinese world fought amongst themselves in shifting alliances. This era of prolonged turbulence is usually labelled the 'warring states period'. It provided the context for the works of two of China's most enduring intellectual giants: Confucius (on political and social philosophy) and Sun Tzu (on statecraft and the art of war). Ultimately the Qin kingdom began to prevail, progressively defeating or securing the allegiance of the others. In 221 BC, the Qin leader proclaimed himself the first emperor of the Qin dynasty. Ironically, the Qin were the least Chinese of the feuding kingdoms. With a territory that straddled the western or inland flank of the other Chinese communities, the Qin gene pool was heavily contaminated by 'barbarian' elements from beyond the Yellow River.

Despite the handicap of suspect ethnicity, the Qin reunified China after centuries of civil war. Moreover, the first Qin emperor proved to be both far-sighted and extraordinarily energetic. In a reign of just 17 years, he set about demolishing the existing feudal structure in favour of centralised bureaucracy, introduced standardised weights and measures, established a single currency and a single written language, and linked the several defensive walls the kingdoms had built to repel nomads into the first instalment of the Great Wall of China. He also moved militarily against the nomads in the north and northwest and endeavoured to occupy the territories thus acquired to prevent re-infiltration. His armies also went south and southeast to accelerate the assimilation of these populations into China proper. The people of these areas, the southern one-third or so of modern China, were generally ethnically Chinese but had, to that point, remained outside the orbit of the dynasties north of the Yangzi River.

The first Qin emperor died in 208 BC and within three years, with the imperial treasury depleted by the cost of the military campaigns, the dynasty collapsed. The Chinese in the south resisted assimilation. The nomad tribes to the north and northwest, emulating the Chinese, confederated for the first time under one leader (Maodun) and became a vastly more formidable security challenge to China proper.

For a few years China flirted with a re-enactment of the warring states era during the Zhou dynasty. On this occasion, fortunately, a dominant player emerged quickly enough to consolidate the Qin gains, with Han Gaodi proclaimed first emperor of the Han dynasty in 202 BC.

The first half of the Han dynasty, a period of roughly two centuries, witnessed the first full flowering of Chinese power and influence in East Asia. Blessed by a succession of able and durable emperors, notably Han Wudi, 170–87 BC, the Han empire expanded hugely to the north, south and, especially, west. After nearly half a century of belligerent coexistence with the nomads of the north and northwest, Han emperors began a century of systematic expansion, both to secure the heartland (that is, to bring all ethnically Chinese people securely under the emperor's sway) and to control as much of the periphery from which the security of the heartland could be threatened.

The Xiongnu (or Mongols) were the first priority. Co-existence was abandoned in 129 BC, and Chinese forces drove the Xiongnu away from regions adjacent to Chinese communities to areas north of the Gobi Desert. China also drove west to contest Xiongnu control of the overland trade routes (collectively dubbed the

'Silk Road'). Thirty years on, the Chinese dominated a broad finger of territory stretching all the way into modern Tajikistan and Uzbekistan. Not only did China thereby gain control of the lucrative but still underdeveloped trade with India, Persia and what would soon become the Roman Empire, it deprived the Xiongnu of the wealth and status that flowed from performing this function.

With the balance of power in central Asia shifting to China, the Xiongnu split into two kingdoms (inner and outer Mongolia) with inner Mongolia formally acknowledging Han supremacy in 51 BC and actually becoming an ally for more than 50 years from 43 BC.

This preoccupation with the Mongols did not preclude other imperial ventures. The Han spent a costly decade (128–118 BC) conquering and occupying the Korean Peninsula, and the north of modern Vietnam, in addition to forcefully requiring the peoples of south and southwestern China to re-join the motherland.

The cost of sustaining these territorial gains, of protecting the aura of a state not to be challenged and of subordinating all domestic claims on government resources to this objective proved unsustainable. Over the 200 years of the later Han dynasty, in an uneven but inexorable process, the Han Empire shrank back to where it had started and even beyond. Containing rebellious Xiongnu thousands of kilometres from the Chinese capital required another debilitating military campaign in 73–89 AD. Each of these efforts made political consensus on the next more improbable. Korea and Vietnam proved to be fiercely resistant to incorporation into greater China, and eternally vigilant for openings to cast the Chinese out.

The Han dynasty finally succumbed in 220 AD and China reverted for another 350 years to several kingdoms vying for dominance over a shadow of the former empire, indeed with much of northern China, the original heartland, occupied by the 'barbarian' Xiongnu. This Xiongnu occupation provoked a mass migration to south of the Yangzi River, an experience that seemingly did little to diminish the animosity southern Chinese felt toward their cousins in the north.

China's second rise to undisputed pre-eminence came under the Tang dynasty (581–907). Scholars debate which of the two—Han China or Tang China—should be regarded as the greater (northerners tend to identify with Han, southerners with Tang) and, with so many potential indices of 'greatness', it is an issue that is certain to remain open.

As was the case for the Han, the foundations for the Tang dynasty were laid by the then most ethnically suspect of the contending kingdoms that occupied China north of the Yellow River. This kingdom ultimately conquered its rival to the south and reunified China under the Sui dynasty. Though relatively short-lived (581–618), the Sui emperors relied heavily on imperial expansion to underpin their authority. Apart from once again compelling the incorporation of the southern Chinese, the external focus was the nomads to the North. Unlike the Qin and Han dynasties six hundred years earlier, the Sui deferred tackling the Xiongnu (Mongols) and focused on the Manchurian tribes to the northeast and the adjacent Koguryo people of North Korea. The Sui fared reasonably well against the Manchurian nomads but failed repeatedly in 612–615 against Koguryo, squandering their military forces, exhausting the treasury, and provoking internal rebellion in the process.

The strongman that emerged from the rebellion founded the Tang dynasty in 618. The first two Tang emperors were obliged to consolidate the home front and to rely on diplomacy and trade to divide and contain nomad incursions. In addition to the Manchus and the Mongols, this threat included a new third player: the tribes of Tibet. Still, the accomplishments of the earlier Han dynasty loomed as the benchmark of dynastic greatness. Eventually the Tang mobilised and moved to regain control of the trade routes in central Asia, pushing the Mongols to the north and the Tibetans to the south. Within 20 years, China's armies again controlled a vast bulb of territory extending into central Asia, although the fact that this territory was connected to China proper by a relatively narrow band of territory perhaps 2000 km long constituted a significant strategic weakness. With success in the west, the Tang diverted their energies to the Koguryo in 645 but, like the Sui, failed in two major assaults. Success against Koguryo did not come until 668, and included the first significant military clash, at sea in 660, between China and Japan. To this point, the various Japanese warlords (Japan as a unitary state still lay one thousand years into the future) had paid insincere homage to successive Chinese emperors and essentially avoided any significant interaction beyond trade. Seemingly, however, the prospect of Chinese control of the whole Korean Peninsula was sufficiently alarming to cause at least some of the Japanese warlords to abandon this longstanding strategy.

Before the costly success in Korea, the Tang were forced to respond to a major Mongol attack in 657 on their newly regained territories in Central Asia. This challenge was successfully repulsed and consolidated an empire that now extended from the eastern extremities of the Persian Empire to the Pacific. After the Mongols, it was the turn of the Tibetans, who swept into China's central Asian territories in 670 and remained for decades a serious rival for control of these territories. Later in the century, various Mongol groups, occasionally in alliance with Tibetan tribes, necessitated major military campaigns in the distant territories, as did rebellion in Manchuria.

Despite these endless challenges, the power and influence of Tang China was without precedent during the seventh century and well into the eighth century. The Tang capital of Chang'an in central China lured the business, cultural, intellectual and political elites from all over the world. Sinocisation, whether imposed or accidental, took place on a scale without precedent in China's history. And China was itself shaped by its deep exposure to cultures in central North Asia, Asia, Persia and India, as well as to those of Southern China and the northern fringes of Southeast Asia.

Eventually, however, the focus and determination required to build and then protect its empire began to fade. The relentless challenges from within (from peoples who resented invariably heavy-handed Chinese domination) and from without (from those envious of China's wealth and power) sapped the resources of the state and the fortitude of the wider populace. Governance became more difficult as the powerful military became a significant political actor and as the fruits of imperial success offered the Chinese political elite other diverting pursuits. Most particularly, perhaps, the careful attention to determining strategic priorities and avoiding simultaneous challenges on distant fronts began to wane. Over the decades 720–750, China was preoccupied with Tibetan challenges to its control of central Asia, but failed until 747 to engineer a decisive engagement. Having secured at least a respite from the Tibetan tribes, it would appear that Chinese forces drifted westward, possibly without a clear mandate from the centre, eventually clashing with an Arab army in the vicinity of Samarkand in 751. The Chinese were defeated, not least because some of the 'allied' nomad forces in their army defected to the Arab side. In the same year, another Tang army was defeated in Manchuria and a third in northern Thailand. The Tang had lost that invaluable aura of invincibility and the determination to prevail at all costs. Even if the centre was disposed to mount the effort needed to recover the losses, it was prevented from doing so by rebellion at home. In December 755, the general who had lost in Manchuria (An Lushan) attempted a coup d'état. Government and rebel forces fought for the next seven years, displaying an even-handed disregard for the interests of the general public. The rebels actually got so far as to occupy the imperial capital at Chang'an in 757. Prejudices were also indulged, including the massacre of foreign merchants by government forces, which did little to enhance China's longer-term economic interests.

The power struggle at the centre required thinning the ranks of the forces elsewhere in the empire. The Tibetans and the tribes of northern central Asia soon ended Chinese control in the West. The Tibetans also struck at Chinese territory in the southwest and briefly occupied the Tang capital at Chang'an in 793, as Chinese rebel forces had done 36 years earlier.

Government forces eventually prevailed over the rebels in 762/63 and the Tang dynasty lingered on for another 140 years. But it was a pale shadow of its former self, presiding increasingly feebly over the Chinese heartland (albeit with significant gaps in the south and southwest of modern China) and, while still a player of some consequence, lacking decisive influence in central Asia,

Manchuria, Korea and Vietnam. Starting in 875, another decade of internal rebellion proved terminal, with a bandit who had graduated to a warlord assassinating the Tang emperor in 904 and setting up his own successor dynasty in 907.

Tibet remained the most formidable adversary but progressively engaged in its own imperial overreach, accumulating more enemies than it could manage and dissipating its energies in prolonged military campaigns, not only against China to the East, but increasingly against Arabs to the West and the Urghurs to the North. The Tibetan empire collapsed in 866, never to be revived.

The next four centuries saw a curious inversion of the historical pattern in Chinese history. There was the characteristic 'shakedown period' (some 50 years) following the demise of Tang, with a clutch of warlords in south and central China and a number of self-proclaimed 'dynasties' in the north, all of which were led by 'barbarians' whose presence the later Tang emperors had either found convenient or been forced to accept. In due course, one of the southern warlords prevailed over the others and established the Song dynasty in 960. In the north, the competing non-Chinese dynasties distilled into two: the Liao directly to the north and the Xi Xia to the northwest.

The Song had inherited a depleted treasury and suppressed whatever pretensions to empire they may have had. Occasional aspirations at least to dislodge the barbarians in the north came to naught and the Song were defeated in two major wars with these regimes, one in the 1030s and the second 50 years later in the 1080s.[2] As a practical matter, for most of the eleventh century, the Song purchased security against the Liao through tribute, accepting a subordinate status. In 1114, northern Manchurians overran the Liao. The Song joined in, hoping to share the spoils with the new regime—the Jin. In the event, the Jin expanded south to the Yellow River, took the Song capital at Kaifeng and imposed much the same status on Song China as had the Liao.

Historians have marked this discontinuity by relabelling the Song era, following this further diminution of the Chinese state, as the Southern Song.

Despite these peculiar circumstances, China continued to flourish under the Song, particularly in economic terms, and to confirm China's status as a major trading power in East and Southeast Asia and beyond to the Middle East. Another century (roughly the thirteenth century) passed until circumstances

---

2   It is striking to note the scale of the warfare that China was capable of a thousand years ago. In both these wars it is believed that the Song dynasty raised an army of in excess of 1 million. At about the same time (1066 to be exact), on the other side of the world, the Normans invaded and occupied England with 7000 men. See Andrew R. Wilson, 'War and the East', address to the Foreign Policy Research Institute's History Institute for Teachers conference on 'Teaching Military History: Why and How', 29–30 September 2007, available at <http://www.fpri.org/education/teachingmilitaryhistory/>, accessed 24 June 2009.

again conspired to revive Chinese aspirations of complete unification. This time it was the Mongols under Chinggis Khan that promised to re-arrange the order in East Asia to China's eventual advantage. Chinggis, already in control of Xinjiang and the now impotent Tibet, invaded and occupied the Xi Xia kingdom in 1209, and then attacked Jin in 1211.[3] Despite initial successes, he lost interest and spent the rest of his life (he died in 1227) conquering most of the known world to the west. His successors, however, renewed Mongol interest in China. In 1228, the Mongols again attacked Jin, occupying roughly half of it, completing the task in 1233 with Song forces as allies.

The Song-Mongol alliance was short-lived. Song attempts to regain some of the former Jin territories provoked the Mongol leadership. The Mongols, of course, were the best military strategists of their day and recognised that China, with its already formidable and culturally alien population, would not be your average conquest. Accordingly, they opened their campaign in an unusually indirect fashion, with Kublai Khan (a grandson of Chinggis) invading and occupying Nanzhou, a large kingdom to the south of China proper and west of Vietnam, in 1252. Succession problems among the Mongols deferred the invasion of China until 1258, and interrupted the campaign in 1259–60, but the Mongol assault was relentless. Kublai proclaimed himself emperor of China, and head of the Yuan dynasty, in 1271, although it was not until 1279 that all Song resistance was eliminated.

China was again reunified, albeit under foreign leadership, three hundred years after the formal demise of the Tang. Kublai was not content with ruling China. He took the title of 'Emperor of all under Heaven' as literally as any of his Chinese predecessors and considered unacceptable any neighbouring state that did not submit unambiguously to his authority. In addition, of course, with Chinggis' vast conquests now divided up and still ruled by his descendents, his extended family set some pretty high performance standards in this regard. The Mongols had pressured the Koguryo in Northern Korea since they conquered the neighbouring Jin kingdom in 1233, and in 1258, with the invasion of China seemingly imminent, the Koguryo submitted to the Mongol Court in Beijing. Kublai drove a hard bargain, extracting a debilitating annual tribute from the Koguryo.

Kublai expected the same of Japan, even though these islands had to that time fallen outside China's sphere of imperial interest. The Japanese rejected

---

3   From 1949, the People's Republic of China was to insist that Tibet had been an inalienable part of China since 1206 when it came under the control of the Mongols who then brought it into China when they established the Yuan dynasty. See Eliot Sperling, *The Tibet-China Conflict: History and Polemics*, Policy Studies, no. 7, East-West Center, Washington, DC, 2004, available at <http://www.eastwestcenter.org/fileadmin/stored/pdfs/PS007.pdf>, accessed 24 June 2009.

diplomatic overtures and, with the help of the weather, repulsed two full-scale Mongol-Korean seaborne invasions, one in 1274 and the second in 1280. A third invasion fleet, built up from 1283 was never used. Kublai died in 1294.

In addition to Japan, Kublai detected shortcomings in the submissiveness of several kingdoms in Southeast Asia. But, in campaigns against the Burmese, the Lao, the Thai and the Vietnamese, the Mongols were either defeated or victory was disproportionately costly. Kublai even sent an armada to secure the submission of kingdoms in Java and Sumatra that controlled the trade routes through the archipelago, but his forces were caught up in a local power struggle, out-manoeuvred and sent packing.

The Yuan dynasty survived Kublai's death by 70 years, until 1368, but its control over China, as well as Mongol dominance over the whole of central Asia to China's west, eroded continuously. The stresses on Mongol authority were compounded by the bubonic plague which devastated both the Mongol heartland and China in the 1320s. Roughly a third of China's population, estimated at about 120 million, is believed to have died. Soon after the plague, Southern China descended into the chaos of competing rebel groups, with a warlord eventually emerging with sufficient forces to defeat his major rivals and then to march against Beijing. The Mongol court decamped and fled into the steppes, with its armed forces largely intact. The victorious rebel leader proclaimed himself the first emperor of the Ming dynasty in 1368.

The Ming dynasty endured for 276 years, until 1644, and followed an all too familiar cycle: energetic expansion that restored China's status (and territory) to Tang levels; maturity and defence of the empire; and finally, decades of erosion.

Two energetic warrior emperors, both with a highly developed sense of Chinese superiority, dominated the first 60 years or so. China's empire expanded back into Manchuria, Northern Vietnam and Tibet. The huge area of Yunnan in Southwest China was occupied and then settled by large numbers of Han Chinese around 1390, bringing it securely into the Chinese heartland for the first time. Between them, the two emperors mounted eight major campaigns against the Mongols, but did not achieve any durable outcomes. Finally, the Ming pushed the empire back into central Asia but wisely stopped well short of the boundaries established by the Tang, thereby simplifying control over their lines of communication and supply to these distant territories.[4]

---

4   One potentially serious challenge to Ming rule evaporated in the icy wastes of central Asia during the winter of 1405–1406. Tamerlane, a Tatar from the region of Samarkand, spent the second half of the fourteenth century in non-stop combat and in building an empire that extended from New Delhi to Ankara and north of the Black, Caspian and Aral Seas to the vicinity of Moscow. Tamerlane was not related to Genghis Khan, but proclaimed that he was following in his footsteps (even though he spent much of his time conquering the mini-empires that Genghis had allocated to his descendants). Similarly, Tamerlane was not Muslim but took great pride in being 'the sword of Islam', despite devoting most of his energy to conquering Islamic leaders in

In a potentially significant new development for China, the Ming built a blue-water fleet and dispatched it on six expeditions to Southeast Asia, India and the East coast of Africa over the period 1405–21.[5] There is little evidence that China had abruptly developed an appreciation of the strategic potential of seapower. Rather, the fleet is perhaps better seen as an indulgence to the emperor's vanity, to expose more peoples to the magnificence of the Ming and to break Han/Tang records on the number of states (or foreign communities) that could be recorded, however misleadingly, as having paid tribute and acknowledged Ming superiority.

Following the death of the second warrior emperor in 1424, Ming emperors became more subdued and, necessarily, fiscally responsible. Vietnam liberated itself from Chinese occupation in 1427 and the loss was allowed to stand. The Mongols remained the key security preoccupation for most of the next two centuries. The Mongols' assertiveness, when they were united, ebbed and surged while the undercurrent of Chinese distaste for engagement with them of any kind, and periodic decisions to stop trade or devalue the terms of trade, ensured intermittent war.

It was noted above that the patchwork of rival warlords on the islands of Japan had long had an instinctive preference to keep the Chinese at arm's length, even to the point in 660 of trying (unsuccessfully) to help the Koguryo kingdom of northern Korea to resist a Tang invasion. This preference was indulged by the Chinese who always looked to the west and to armies rather than east to the sea and naval power. This pattern was broken by the Yuan dynasty (Kublai Khan) and its repeated attempts to invade Japan in the thirteenth century. Against the background of these pointers, toward the end of the sixteenth century, the foundations were laid for a defining feature of contemporary East Asia—the deep antagonism between China and Japan.

As in China, the internal unity of the Japanese communities had been an inconsistent affair for centuries, but in 1590 a warrior called Hideyoshi brought

---

places like Damascus, Baghdad, Isfahan and Shiraz. Tamerlane is credited with having 'saved' Western Europe in 1402 by routing the forces of the Ottoman leader Bayazid near Ankara. Bayazid had already defeated the best army (the fourth crusade) that the fractured leadership of Western Europe could mount against him. Tamerlane, however, took seriously intelligence reports that little of value lay to the West of Ankara, deciding instead to indulge an ambition that he had nursed for many years, namely, to conquer the biggest empire of all, China. At the age of 74, he succumbed to a cold en route to Beijing, somewhere in the eastern regions of modern Kazakhstan. Tamerlane had never lost a campaign, but he would have encountered a mobilised China under the second Ming emperor who was an energetic warrior prince busily engaged in extending the boundaries of China's empire. See Justin Marozzi, *Tamerlane: Sword of Islam, Conqueror of the World,* Da Capo Press, Cambridge, MA, 2006.

5   An enterprising retired British submariner has argued that elements of one of these fleets almost certainly 'discovered' America (not to mention Antarctica and Australia) more than 50 years ahead of Christopher Columbus. See Gavin Menzies, *1421: The Year China Discovered America,* Harper Collins Publishers, New York, 2003.

all four of the main islands under his control. Hideyoshi appeared to have been cut from the same cloth as Kublai. Responding to a congratulatory note from the King of Korea, he sought safe passage through Korea for a Japanese force that would conquer China. The stunned Koreans equivocated, only to be invaded by Japan in 1592. Within two months, 200 000 Japanese troops were at the Yalu River. An exhausted Ming assembled yet another large force and, together with the Koreans, pushed the Japanese back to an enclave around Pusan at the foot of the peninsula. Years of negotiations on a settlement ensued until Hiroyoshi sent a second invasion force to Korea in 1597. This time the Koreans defeated the Japanese single-handedly, although their entire nation had been ravaged by the armies of both major contenders.

By this time, the authority of the Ming had begun to unravel. Rebel groups had sprung up in the south of China and pressures from the periphery—the Mongols, the central Asian tribes, and the Burmese—persisted. A new challenge emerged in Manchuria. The Jurchens in northern Manchuria, provoked by centuries of Chinese domination, had become strong and ambitious, and moved south to the boundaries of China proper in the early 1600s. They invaded China in 1618. During this time, perceived Korean loyalty to the Ming was remembered and repaid in 1636 with a Manchurian invasion. It took 40 years to subdue all the Ming forces, but the Manchurians did not wait that long. They occupied Beijing in 1644 and proclaimed the Qing dynasty.In their first one hundred years, the Qing roughly doubled the territory under direct Chinese control compared to the Ming at the height of their imperial expansion. Naturally enough, the Qing brought the whole of greater Manchuria into the empire, along with the Korean Peninsula. They also expanded dramatically to the northwest, invading and this time occupying modern Mongolia. They moved much further west than had the Ming, occupying all of modern Xinjiang and holding it determinedly against the Western Mongols.

The Western Mongols proved a persistent threat, manoeuvring widely over the expanses of central Asia, including into Tibet until the Qing secured a decisive victory near the Tibetan capital, Lhasa. The Qing annexed Eastern Tibet in the 1720s, but a later rebellion resulted in a full-scale Qing invasion of Tibet in 1751.

With central Asia relatively secure, even though the Qing found it necessary to station significant forces among these alien populations, there was spare capacity to contest Burmese aspirations to empire. As before (under the Mongols), a five year campaign (1765–69) proved inconclusive, but shortly afterwards the Thai were strong enough to squash Burmese aspirations. In an interesting new departure, perceived Nepalese interference in Tibetan affairs, which the Qing suspected had British support, resulted in the invasion of Nepal in 1792 and the extraction of submission and tribute from the King.

From the beginning of the eighteenth century, European intrusion into what had been China's exclusive preserve for millennia began in earnest. Europeans (especially the Portuguese and the Dutch) had been around for two hundred years, but had readily been confined to activities that rarely impinged on the Chinese leadership. The European intrusion was neither casual nor accidental, but instead driven by a gathering re-ordering of global wealth and power in favour of Europe on the back of the Industrial Revolution. This underlying transformation remained invisible to a Chinese leadership whose vision and curiosity was confined to an area of the earth defined by their predecessors over two thousand years earlier.

The issue of contention was trade, and trade occupied a very different space in the minds of Europeans and Chinese. For Europeans, international trade was accepted as a basic instrument to develop national wealth and wellbeing, as well as a rewarding activity for an important class in the wider population. It was presumed that foreign communities could be pressured, or even coerced if necessary, to engage in 'fair' 'trade. For the Chinese, timeless practice had pigeon-holed trade as a key tool of diplomacy and statecraft—and as a tool essentially to be wielded by the emperor alone. The notion of broad and uninhibited engagement in international trade was quite alien and, under Confucian values, which place trade and merchants near the bottom of the social order, deeply suspect.

The Qing response to the lengthening queue of European and American traders was to require that all international trade be conducted through one location—Canton, in the deep South—and be vetted through a Chinese guild. Direct access to Chinese officials was prohibited. This severe constraint on profitable trade not only frustrated the Europeans but came to be viewed by the British, the emergent superpower, as demeaning and unacceptable. The British took the lead to convert China to the contemporary Western conception of trade, although, disgracefully, a more specific driver was to export larger quantities of opium to offset the cost of Chinese tea.

Two British diplomatic overtures, in 1792 and 1816, were shunned by the Qing. Later, in 1839, the Qing decided to suppress the import of opium—an effort that escalated into a confrontation with all foreign traders and their expulsion from Canton. The British responded with a distinctly modest force of gunboats and 4000 troops, but they sent the bulk of this force directly to Tianjin, adjacent to Beijing, and extracted an agreement from the Qing in 1841 to negotiate more liberal arrangements. Both negotiators were penalised by their governments—the Englishman for not getting enough and his Chinese counterpart for giving up too much. But it was the British who followed through on their assessment, assembling a somewhat larger naval force that captured the ports of Ningbo and Shanghai, and sending a land force that fought its way to Nanking before the

Qing capitulated and further liberalised the trade regime. In 1857, the British renewed their military coercion, taking the city of Guangzhou in the South and again landing a force at Tianjin, and thereby extracting further concessions from the Qing, not the least of which was foreign ambassadors in Beijing with rights of access to the Emperor. In an attempt to wind back these concessions, Qing forces trounced the complacent British in Tianjin to which the British, with French assistance, responded by occupying Beijing in 1860 with 20 000 troops.

What is truly remarkable is the extraordinary economy of force needed by the British to compel the Qing to make humiliating concessions and, ultimately, to occupy the Chinese capital. It speaks volumes for the enormity of the gap in military technology that the Europeans had opened up over the Chinese. The mobility of Mongol forces had tested the Chinese for untold centuries, but they had learned to emulate this capability and to supplement it with overwhelmingly large ground forces. However, in the nineteenth century, no degree of sheer mass could offset European technology. In addition, the Qing had entered the now characteristic spiral of decline, with a succession of devastating internal rebellions breaking out from 1850 onwards that sapped the energies of a tired and bewildered dynasty for more than 20 years. China's familiar world had changed dramatically, and threatened to become unrecognisable. The Qing, with a thoroughly obsolete set of instruments of power, could do little more than watch.

There is no evidence that the Europeans or the Americans entertained the option of 'owning' China, despite the acquisition of colonies being the height of fashion at the time. The United States, of course, eschewed colonisation on principle, but was to compromise later in respect of the Philippines. Indeed, having secured from the Qing court arrangements that met their interests, this new cohort of barbarians preferred that the Qing remain in power. The precedent of British India would suggest that China's size was not a complete deterrent, but the Indian Mutiny of 1857 would doubtless have put London in a cautious frame of mind. In addition, the sheer scale of such an undertaking, amplified by an awareness that China was utterly alien in every way and an appreciation of China's long status as the local superpower, probably all contributed to colonisation not even being considered as desirable.

Japan, on the other hand, not only dreamed about conquering China, but also about replicating China's past dominance of Asia, even though that task would now entail dislodging the Western powers. Asian intellectuals were not slow to diagnose the sources of Western strength and to identify the key changes that Asian societies needed to accomplish to regain countervailing power. The Qing attempted some reforms, but only half-heartedly as many of them threatened imperial-style governance. Moreover, as the reach of Qing authority had shrunk dramatically, the reforms took hold unevenly under regional rather than national leadership

Japan had a more fortuitous history in this regard, undergoing a thorough political cleansing in 1868 (the Meiji Restoration) and able to generate a national consensus to copy the West so as to become strong enough to expel the West. This national game plan was implemented with a thoroughness bordering on fanaticism that came to be seen as a defining national characteristic.

Within 25 years, in 1894, Japan and China had declared war on each other over control of Korea. Japan crushed Qing forces and extended its conquests beyond Korea into southern Manchuria, including the Liaodong Peninsula that commands the sea adjacent to Beijing. Combined Russian, French and German pressure forced Japan to relinquish this peninsula (but not other aspects of a harsh deal struck with the Qing). A decade later, in 1904, Japan sank the Russian fleet stationed at Port Arthur on the peninsula, and then did the same in the Tsushima Strait in 1905 to the naval force that Moscow had dispatched from the Baltic Sea to restore its position.

The ensuing settlement, brokered by the United States, accepted that Korea was essentially a Japanese protectorate and confirmed Russian claims to North Manchuria. A few years later, in 1910, Japan put Korea's status beyond doubt by annexing it, while its forces in Manchuria, seemingly just loosely controlled by Tokyo, menaced the other nations (including Britain and the United States) pursuing economic interests in this region.

Humiliation at the hands of the Japanese came on top of burgeoning activities by the Europeans and Americans throughout coastal China. The famous (anti-foreigner) Boxer rebellion at the end of the nineteenth century gave way to a more coherent nationalist movement in the south led by Sun Yat-sen. Sun eventually cut a deal with the military commander the Qing emperor had dispatched to crush his movement. Faced with this joint opposition, the Qing emperor abdicated in the commander's favour in 1912, bringing 268 years of Manchu rule to an end. But this time there was an aspiration to also change the governance of China. There was no aspirant emperor, and an imperial system dating back four thousand years also came to an end. Unsurprisingly, this transformation was to be a prolonged and untidy affair (and, in the opinion of some, more apparent than real given the ultimate emergence of Mao Zedong) and China's steep decline relative to the other major powers since the end of the eighteenth century continued for another 50 years.

Japan's belligerence—fuelled by victory over the Russians, an alliance with the British, and European preoccupation with their war of 1914–18—intensified, imposing an agreement on the new leader of the Republic of China in 1915 that constituted a further, and extraordinary, infringement of China's sovereignty. Japanese gains in Korea, Manchuria and China proper (particularly the Shandong Peninsula taken over from the Germans) were consolidated by the Treaty of Versailles in 1919, even though it was China that had contributed troops to the winning coalition in Europe and had hoped for some reward.

Sun Yat-sen's efforts to hold China together after 1912 faced the familiar epidemic of warlordism following the demise of a dynasty. In March 1920, the new Communist government in Moscow offered some support by voluntarily surrendering some of its privileges in Manchuria—an extremely popular gesture that reflected well on Sun. Moscow's reasoning was probably dominated by the calculation that a coherent China would be the best way to contain Japan which had humiliated it in 1904–1905 and which continued vigorously to contest Russian (now Soviet) dominance of Manchuria. Aside from helping to form the Chinese Communist Party (CCP) in the early 1920s, Moscow followed up its gesture in Manchuria through a willingness to assist Sun in improving the effectiveness of his armed forces, led by General Chiang Kai-shek. Chiang's forces ultimately prevailed over the warlords and his Kuomintang movement (Sun Yat-sen had died in 1925) was officially recognised as the government of China in October 1928.

Along the way, Chiang had decided that his increasingly popular Communist allies, led by Mao Zedong, posed a threat to his leadership. He ordered a bloody purge of communists in 1927. The civil war between the communists and the nationalists that ensued consumed the next 20 years. Japan's long-heralded invasion of China, which finally kicked off in 1937 and, in a conspicuously brutal campaign, resulted in the occupation of most of the eastern regions of the country, brought about a reluctant and largely ineffective truce. China's civil war resumed after Japan surrendered unconditionally in August 1945, with Mao and Chiang Kai-shek competing vigorously to be the 'authority' that accepted the surrender of the various Japanese forces in China. Ultimately, the Communist forces prevailed in 1949, with the remnant Nationalist forces finding sanctuary on Taiwan and in northern Burma. On 1 October 1949, Mao Zedong proclaimed the establishment of the People's Republic of China (PRC).

Although we have a great deal of distracting information on China's third descent from empirical grandeur and pre-eminence in Asia, the general pattern is very similar to the decline in the Han and Tang eras. But this time there was a curious difference. The empire was not lost. Even though China had fallen into impotence over the period 1800–1950, the extent of the territory internationally reorganised as China, after the Qing fell in 1911 and until Mao took over nearly 40 years later, was very nearly as great as the Han, Tang or Qing dynasties at their height.

Map 1: Early Han Dynasty

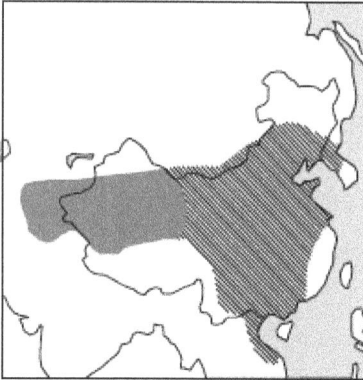

■ Chinese presence was primarily military

Map 2: Late Han Dynasty

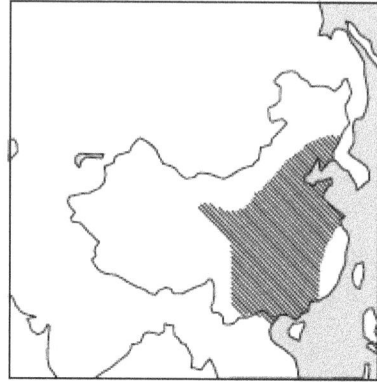

Map 3: Early Tang Dynasty

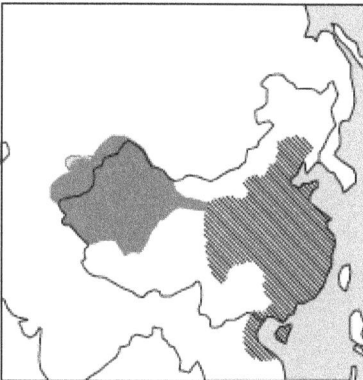

■ Chinese presence was primarily military

Map 4: Late Tang Dynasty

Map 5: Early Ming Dynasty

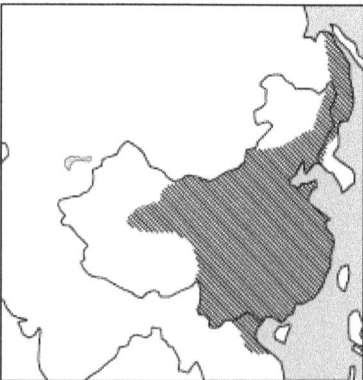

Map 6: Late Ming Dynasty

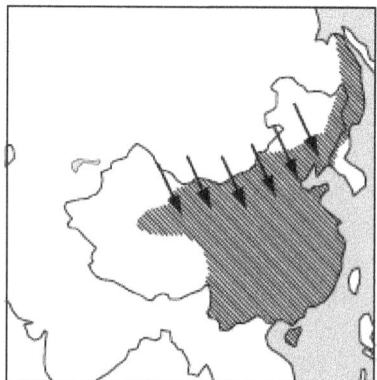

(Arrows denote extensive foreign incursions)

Map 7: Early Qing Dynasty   ## Map 8: Late Qing Dynasty

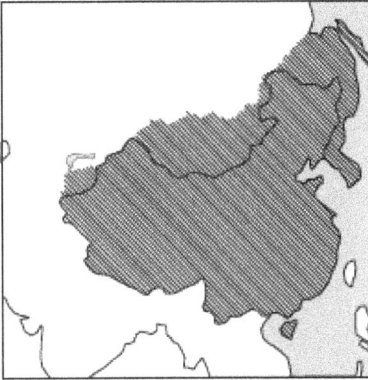

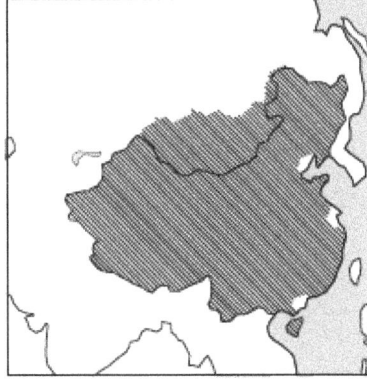

(*Source for Maps 1–8*: Michael D. Swaine and Ashley J. Tellis, *Interpreting China's Grand Strategy: Past, Present, and Future*, Monograph Report, RAND Corporation, Santa Monica, CA, 2000, Maps 4a–4h on pp. 41–44, available at <http://www.rand.org/pubs/monograph_reports/MR1121/>, accessed 16 November 2009).

In 1913, the new Republic of China had to accept that Outer Mongolia and the central Asian region of Xinjiang would be autonomous regions (to protect Russian and British interests respectively). But China retained formal sovereignty over these areas, as well as Tibet and Manchuria. As a practical matter, Japan and Russia had essentially split Manchuria away from China, but Japan's defeat in 1945 and Russia's (by then the Soviet Union) limited bargaining power in East Asia relative to the United States in the aftermath of the Second World War saw this region also returned to China.

The vicissitudes of great power politics conspired, literally, to donate to today's China the empire that it had repeatedly striven at prodigious cost to acquire. Part of the explanation lies in the growing formalisation of international relations, and the strong attachment to clear borders as a pre-requisite for order and stability. A further consideration was that when the United States emerged from the Second World War as the dominant power, Asia was a subordinate interest to Europe and a region in which the priority was to strip Japan of capacities to re-emerge as a dominant player. In addition, there was already sufficient apprehension about the Soviet Union to make strengthening its position in east and central Asia generally unattractive to the United States. Finally, Britain had all but decided that its imperial days were over and was not inclined to press its interests in Tibet. China benefited from the fallout of these developments and strategic judgements.

The tribute system

The extraordinary durability of imperial China, and the fact that so much of this remarkable national journey is reasonably well documented, has naturally produced in the Chinese something approaching reverence of the lessons of history. One might be forgiven for thinking that, over the course of four thousand years, China has prospered and prevailed in every imaginable circumstance and, presumably, made every mistake and error of judgement that it is possible to make. Thus, looking to past episodes for guidance on what to do and not do continues to be an important element in framing China's policy options in addressing today's challenges.

The question for many scholars of China has been whether this extraordinary history either reflects or has etched into Chinese minds attitudes and presumptions that help to explain China's political behaviour today and/or which offer clues about the longer-term ambitions of the Chinese leadership. Most of these scholars look for answers to these questions in the so-called *tribute system*, a term used to describe the essence of the arsenal of techniques of statecraft that China developed and used in every conceivable combination to manage its empire as cost-effectively as possible. It was, in other words, essentially the art of *Realpolitik*, Chinese style. The term derives from the view that the strongest and most consistent characteristic the Chinese projected was the belief that it had no equals in the universe known to it, that all other communities were 'inferior' and that all its international dealings and relationships should reflect this fact.

Swaine and Tellis characterised the tribute system in the following terms:

> For a strong imperial state, the traditional tributary relationship served many practical, political, economic, and cultural purposes: It reaffirmed the applicability to Chinese and non-Chinese alike of China's hierarchical and sinocentric system of political and social values and thereby legitimized the entire Confucian order, it provided an avenue for regular diplomatic communication between the Chinese court and foreign rulers, and it served as a convenient and durable basis for mutually beneficial economic relations between China and foreign states, thereby increasing, in many instances, China's leverage over those states. In addition tributary relations also gave recipient periphery states important legitimacy, status, and leverage within their own subregion, by providing significant economic benefits and a form of political recognition by the dominant power in East Asia. Moreover, tributary status often, although not always, implied Chinese diplomatic and military protection of the vassal state against domestic usurpers or foreign nontributary states, as noted above.

When possible, strong Chinese imperial regimes generally sought to ground the tributary and trade relationship in a genuinely hierarchical power structure based on a clear position of military superiority. Under such circumstances, periphery powers were often pressured, enticed or coerced by strong and wealthy imperial Chinese regimes to accept a more clearly defined status as Chinese vassals that involved specific reciprocal benefits and obligations. Local leaders were usually allowed to retain their positions and rule their lands as they wished, provided they kept the peace, accepted symbols of (Chinese) overlordship, and assisted (Chinese) armies when called on. They would also often receive generous gifts, subsidies, and trade concessions from the Chinese court, ostensibly as an expression of the benevolence and generosity of the emperor, but more accurately to ensure continued loyalty and support. Such gifts and concessions (along with various diplomatic ploys) were often used by a strong regime to foment hostilities among nomadic groups and to prevent the formation of nomadic confederations. In some instances, and particularly during the early period of contact with imperialist powers in the mid 19th century, a compliant vassal state (such as Korea at that time) would also agree to avoid foreign relations with states other than China. In return, the Chinese state often assumed a level of responsibility for the security of the vassal, especially against external attack.[6]

Warren Cohen offers a not dissimilar view:

It was during [the Han dynasty] that the Chinese developed practices for managing foreign affairs traditionally referred to as the tributary system, a system of enormous *political* importance to Chinese ruling elites and of great *economic* importance to those regimes that accepted tributary status. Under the system, non-Chinese—'barbarian'—states accepted a nominally subordinate place in the Chinese imperial order. They demonstrated this subordination by sending missions to the Chinese court and paying homage to the Chinese ruler to whom they presented acceptable gifts. They often left what amounted to hostages at the Chinese court, usually members of their ruling families. In return they received gifts from the emperor, often more valuable than those they had submitted, and opportunities for private trade. Obviously, the greater the Chinese need for the submission of the tributary state, the greater its potential threat to Chinese security or its importance as an ally—the greater the value of the goods sent back with the tribute mission. The system appears to have been expensive for the Chinese, but the symbolic submission of the barbarian state was more palatable

---

6   Swaine and Tellis, *Interpreting China's Grand Strategy: Past, Present and Future*, pp. 69–70.

politically than outright appeasement and less problematic than endless warfare on the periphery. To the barbarians, ritual submission was the price they grudgingly paid in exchange for Chinese bribes and access to trade. Yu Ying-shih, the leading authority on Han foreign relations, argues that the tribute system was a net loss to China at the state level although individual Chinese profited.[7]

Elsewhere in the same study, Cohen observes:

> In its most obvious form, a foreign ruler paid homage to the Chinese emperor by sending an embassy or appearing himself at the Chinese court. Once there he would present gifts to the emperor and very likely leave a hostage or hostages, perhaps even his son. In return the Chinese would lavish gifts upon him, more often than not of a value in excess of those received, and permit private trade. The tributary systems was at once a formula for diplomatic intercourse, a symbol of peace and friendship between unequal sovereign states—a nonaggression pact or even alliance, and a vehicle for trade relations. The Chinese received acknowledgment of their superiority, at least nominal, and assurances of the vassal states' good behavior. The tribute bearers obtained insurance against Chinese aggression, the possibility of protection against other enemies, access to Chinese goods, and a significant profit through the exchange of presents itself. It was a system the Chinese found useful when they lacked the will or the power to crush or occupy another state. But it was an expensive system and there were always those at court who argued (with occasional success) that it was cheaper to fight or even ignore a given group of foreigners. The existence of the tributary system should not be allowed to conceal the fact that the Chinese were masterful practitioners of *Realpolitik*.[8]

Both these characterisations of the tribute system support the more pithy observation that 'neighbouring polities sent missions to the Chinese court to pay deference as an insurance policy against being attacked'.[9] Both also support widespread shorthand characterisations of the Chinese as imbued with a deep sense of superiority over other communities and races and as never abandoning the thought that a comprehensively Sino-centric world order was natural and proper.

China, with the Emperor of all under Heaven at its head, had devised the optimum political and social contract for unity and harmony within. Imposing the same order externally had obvious attractions, but required both the means to do so

---

7   Cohen, *East Asia at the Center*, p. 25.
8   *Cohen, East Asia at the Center*, p. 60.
9   Terrill, *The New Chinese Empire and What It Means for the United States*, p. 36.

and generating the political will to apply these capacities to this purpose. As to the former, China's marked preponderance in strategic weight over all other communities in East Asia meant that powerful leaders could, it seems, always draw on reserves of wealth and resilience that were unmatched in the region. The latter came in the form of strategic imperatives combined with the mission of exposing neighbouring peoples to the Chinese way of doing things; that is, to Sinocise them or to make the periphery as much like China as possible. Under this mindset, where overt subordination to China was seen not simply as advantageous but as the only conceivable basis for harmony and stability, neighbouring polities, necessarily inferior, had duties rather than rights towards the centre (or China) which in and of itself constituted the international system.

To impose and sustain this conception of order was difficult and hugely expensive. It inflicted massive grief on the Chinese as well as the peoples within its reach. It meant that China's emperors could never settle for anything less than absolute power. Power could not be shared. There could be no partner, not even a hierarchy of states in China's orbit.

The fact that the Chinese apparently came to this view, and burnished it so earnestly for so long, is undoubtedly testimony to the magnitude of the economic and technological edge they held over their neighbours for at least the past 2500 years. Through its indigenous efforts supplemented by continuous cross-fertilisation and technology transfer with states near and far, it seems fair to say that, for nearly all of this vast expanse of time, China remained up-to-date and, indeed, sustained an edge in science and technology and its application to economic and military pursuits. In terms of political, economic and social structures and processes, China's sophistication and depth of experience was perhaps even more commanding. Not until the Industrial Revolution in Europe in the eighteenth and nineteenth centuries was China exposed as having missed a decisive transformation in the sources of national power and strategic weight. The imperial system, datable from around 1800 BC, and having endured every imaginable challenge, eventually succumbed because of this strategic oversight. It staggered on for perhaps a century after it became apparent that China was unambiguously backward in this crucial dimension of national power, eventually collapsing in 1911.

It is worth pointing out that, on the two occasions that they were conquered, occupied and ruled by outsiders, their enemies took decades to accomplish this feat. The Mongols took two decades (1258–79) and the Manchurians four decades (1618–58) to completely subdue the forces of the dynasty they attacked (the Song and the Ming respectively). Moreover, it is clear from the discussion above that, for all of the past 2500 years, China accounted for such a decisive slice of the East Asian strategic pie that no alternative centre of gravity for the region emerged or was imaginable. There were extended periods when Heaven itself appeared to lose sight of Chinese superiority. In addition to the 350 years of Mongol and Manchu leadership, for the 329 years of the Song dynasty China's emperors virtually paid tribute to the two nomad kingdoms that occupied all of Northern China and which never lost the capacity to coerce Song China. Even when the country was occupied, however, its conquerors had to step into China's world and rule from within.

China's pretensions to innate superiority could be manipulated to advantage, and they were. Foreigners gathered intelligence on the Imperial Court—the character of the Emperor, the predispositions of his principal advisers, the strength of China's armed forces, the state of the Treasury and so on—to assess how profitable they could make the gesture of tribute.

It is hard to believe that China's leaders remained unaware for very long that being seen as craving even the appearance of subordination set the stage for bad bargains. There are records of the emperors' advisors carefully weighing the tangible and intangible costs and benefits of alternative foreign and security policy settings. Although it is often observed that in many instances China paid a disproportionately heavy price to secure a measure of cooperation from another state, it is hard to believe that China's leaders did not consider it a rational act in the circumstances they found themselves in. Conversely, on the occasions when a state that was clearly not a core security problem for China refused to pay tribute and was invaded, it seems likely that the explanation could be found in assessments of how others would perceive such a refusal, its impact on China's aura of leadership at the time and the potential costs further down the road if others were emboldened to follow the example.

The Imperial legacy

Generations of scholars of post-imperial China have naturally wondered whether China was completely re-inventing itself or adapting ancient attitudes, aims and practices to its new internal and external environments. Where does China think it belongs in the scheme of things? How does it propose, and what is it prepared to do, to get there? Does Beijing have any indicative timetable for this journey? Put in other words, does China have a grand strategy and to what extent is this strategy informed by the past, whether by memories of greatness and of how that greatness was achieved, a yearning to recreate a traditional Sinocentric world order, or by the more limited, if perhaps interim, goal of erasing the so-called 'century of humiliation'?

From 1912 to 1978, the question of China's grand strategy was a rather esoteric interest as a succession of disasters, both inflicted on and by China, kept the country in a state of incoherent weakness. Since the seminal decisions of 1978, however, the question has steadily attracted more interest and acquired greater relevance.

The issue of whether China's contemporary behaviour should be regarded to some significant extent as an echo of the attitudes and perceptions that drove its imperial leadership in the past may be a matter of personal judgement rather than a question that can be addressed analytically.

Writing in the late 1960s, some leading Sinologists concluded that China had broken decisively with its past conceptions of world order. John Fairbank dissected the signature dimension of this world order, the tribute system through which all non-Chinese endorsed and re-inforced Chinese conceptions of superiority and centrality by being seen to pay homage to the emperor, depicting it as a far more practical and less absolute construct than popular myth suggested.[10] The posture of superiority toward non-Chinese, seen as central to the emperor's standing within China and therefore to political and social harmony, was implemented with great flexibility and responsiveness to China's real bargaining power at any particular moment. The terms of tribute were frequently highly advantageous to those seeking the Emperor's blessing. When the system functioned to its full potential, it not only delivered political harmony within China but also organised China's relations with the communities that surrounded it. The thrust of this argument supports the view that the tribute system can be adequately explained as a tool of political management: one does not have to resort to the contention that it is evidence of an attitude deeply engrained in the Chinese psyche.

This deflation of the tribute system fits with the alacrity with which China abandoned the imperial system and the notion of a universal Kingship—the Emperor of all under Heaven—in 1911–12, although the fact that the Qing dynasty was Manchu rather than Chinese doubtless also helped this rejection. Moreover, this went hand in hand with China's embrace of the multi-state system at the end of the nineteenth century. The system of states required that polities engage one and other nominally as equals, the antithesis of the ancient Chinese view that all foreigners were inferior and that, regardless of size, proximity and importance to China, none could engage the Chinese state as an equal or even be informally ranked as more or less important than others to China. This combination of developments led Benjamin Schwartz to contend that China's perceptions of world order had been fundamentally undermined

---

10   John K. Fairbank (ed.), *The Chinese World Order: Traditional China's Foreign Relations,* Harvard University Press, Cambridge, MA, 1968.

in the twentieth century and that any assertions that this ancient wisdom had significant explanatory value for the policies China pursued in the late 1960s or beyond should be viewed sceptically.[11]

This particular view, that today's China could and should be regarded, for analytical purposes, as analogous to any other major player on the international stage, was not, of course, uncontested. Writing in the same volume from the late 1960s, Wang Gungwu insisted that the Chinese sense of superiority is real, that Chinese feel that their history is relevant for all time, and the possibility that, down the road, China will again allow this attitude to shape its external posture should be a matter of concern.[12] More recently, Ross Terrill has devoted an entire book to the same theme, namely, that the ambitions and practices of Communist China's leaders can be shown to be deeply rooted in these ancient traditions.[13]

Without resorting to a personal judgement and, to some extent, anticipating the discussion to follow, several propositions related to this important issue can be advanced with a measure of confidence:

- First, East Asia is rapidly regaining the status in the world economy that it enjoyed for centuries prior to the Industrial Revolution.

- Second, East Asia is trending back to its traditional configuration in which China is the economic, political and military centre of gravity. Japanese and, prospectively, Indian economic power will attenuate Chinese dominance, giving it more the status of the first among equals rather than the marked pre-eminence that appears to have characterised the past.

- Third, China's leadership has consciously pursued policies intended to counter and break down expectations that its worldview is still informed either by revolutionary socialist principles or by the attitudes associated with its imperial past. The objectives of these policies include facilitating commerce and countering instincts among China's neighbours to be nervous about a strong China and to seek reassurance in closer relations with other strong powers, especially the United States.

- Fourth, China's confidence in its culture and history, and, increasingly, in its attractiveness as an economic partner, is palpable. China's leaders are demonstrating that playing in the game of nations at the highest level represents normality for China, and is something that they excel at.

---

11 Benjamin I. Schwartz, 'The Chinese Perception of World Order, Past and Present', in John K. Fairbank, (ed.), *The Chinese World Order: Traditional China's Foreign Relations,* Harvard University Press, Cambridge, 1968, p. 284.

12 Wang Gungwu, 'Early Ming Relations With Southeast Asia: A Background Essay', in John K. Fairbank (ed.), *The Chinese World Order: Traditional China's Foreign Relations,* pp. 34–62.

13 Terrill, *The New Chinese Empire and What It Means for the United States.*

By the late 1990s, that is, thirty years later, analysts had a more stable foundation upon which to base their assessments and projections. For the last two of these three decades China had decisively abandoned revolutionary zeal and Socialist dogma, embracing the market economy, international trade and economic interdependence, and progressively acquiring the attributes of a regular member of the international community (by, for example, signing the Non-Proliferation Treaty (NPT) and joining the World Trade Organization (WTO)). The choice in favour of the market economy discarded one of the basic principles of Socialism, while accepting the prospect of deepening economic interdependence with other nations ran counter to preferences that China had displayed for millennia. The impact of these 1978 decisions was dramatic and by the early 1990s China had flourished into an economic phenomenon that people already sensed would ultimately transform the economic, political and military order, certainly in East Asia if not more broadly.

Chapter 2

The People's Republic of China: Early Foreign and Security Policy Choices

The Mao era

In 1949, Mao Zedong's Communist forces swept their nationalist rivals out of China's heartland—with the remnants taking refuge on Taiwan and in northern Burma—and proclaimed the People's Republic of China (PRC) on 1 October of that year. Beyond superior military skills, the decisive development was that public opinion ultimately swung emphatically in favour of the Communists as more disciplined, less corrupt and less brutal than the Nationalists.

In allied discussions on the postwar order, US President Franklin D. Roosevelt consistently insisted that China had to be brought into the inner circle of major powers, including through granting them a permanent seat on the proposed United Nations Security Council (UNSC). Roosevelt would certainly have presumed a postwar China led by the Kuomintang, but such was the US disillusionment with its erstwhile Chinese allies that, at least initially, Mao's eventual victory did not generate great shock or alarm.

For rather different reasons, the Soviet Union was also disposed to react cautiously. Joseph Stalin was to admit later that he had not assessed China to be 'ripe' for a genuine Marxist revolution (as a pre-industrial state it was theoretically unqualified).[1] His dealings with the Chinese Communists in the 1920s and 1930s had been limited and hesitant, and he had established no rapport whatever with Mao. Stalin had cut a deal with Roosevelt at Yalta to restore Russia's Tsarist-era privileges in Northeast Asia in return for joining the war against Japan after Germany had surrendered, and he judged a Chinese Nationalist government to be more likely than the Communists to accept this arrangement. Moreover, Stalin was aware that some of the Communist leaders in China saw an accommodation with the United States as the surest means to rebuild China's economic strength. Moscow was therefore somewhat ambivalent about the new government in Beijing, initially uncertain about how reliable an asset it could prove to be in the Soviet Union's looming contest with the United States. Like the Americans, Stalin suspected more Chinese Nationalism than

---

1   John Lewis Gaddis, *We Now Know: Rethinking Cold War History*, Oxford University Press, New York, 1997, pp. 70–84.

Communist ideology in Mao's movement—a characteristic that he feared (and the Americans hoped) would make China resistant to direction from Moscow. It would appear that this wariness endured until Beijing, egged on by Moscow, committed forces to the Korean War (1950–53) and codified Chinese-US enmity.

Even though Mao had said in a speech in June 1949 that a Communist China would 'lean' toward the East, engaging with Moscow proved awkward. Mao spent a full two months in Moscow toward the end of 1949, eventually concluding the mutual security pact that he, convinced of US belligerence, craved, but at no point achieving any genuine rapport with Stalin. In some ways, however, Mao gained rather more than a security pact. Stalin eventually appreciated the enormity of the advance for the Communist cause that Mao's victory brought about. He spoke graciously of the possibility that new centres of Marxist-Leninism could take the revolution even further than the Soviet Union could, and invited China to take the lead in promoting the Communist cause in its immediate region.

In the latter months of 1949 and through the first half of 1950, the United States continued to regard Northeast Asia (except for Japan) as a second-order arena. The political leadership had considered drafts of a major assessment (known as NSC-68) of what confronting and containing the Soviet Union would mean for US foreign and security policies. This assessment characterised the Soviet Union as having a 'grand design' of global dimensions, imparting strategic significance to Communist advances anywhere, and calling for major, and indefinite, US rearmament, both nuclear and conventional. In Korea, however, tired of being 'aligned' with a brutal regime in the South and judging reunification by force to be improbable, the United States withdrew its forces in 1949. Washington also anticipated, and was reconciled to, Communist China moving quickly, probably in 1950, to invade Taiwan and completing the victory over the Nationalists.

The United States then put these judgements on the public record, in a speech by US Secretary of State Dean Acheson in January 1950. Acheson all but said that those interests in Northeast Asia that the United States would defend pro-actively began and ended in Japan. Korea and Taiwan were quite explicitly excluded. These developments are thought to have tipped the scales in Stalin's calculations. He endorsed Mao's plans for Taiwan and supported Kim Il-Sung's renewed pressure for authorisation and support to invade South Korea, on the condition that North Korea and, if necessary, China do all the fighting. He made explicit that the direct engagement of Soviet armed forces in combat with US forces was out of the question. Kim suppressed some of these details, probably giving both Stalin and Mao a stronger sense of the other's enthusiasm for the invasion than was in fact the case. With the offensive capacities of his forces bolstered with Soviet-supplied equipment, Kim launched the invasion on 25 June 1950. Four months later, having come within a whisker of complete success,

North Korean forces were being overwhelmed by the US-led coalition and the exact opposite of what Kim had in mind looked inevitable. Stalin refused to budge, telling Mao in plain language that whether or not there would be a US-dominated Korea with US forces on the Yalu River was Mao's choice alone.

Mao, though presumably mindful that Japan's invasion of China had begun with the occupation of Korea, and disposed to come to the aid of the North Koreans, hesitated, incurring intensified pressure from Stalin but also promises of indirect assistance, including the sale of air support equipment.

The UNSC resolution authorising resistance to the North Korea invasion implied strongly that the objective was to drive Communist forces back over the de facto border at the 38th parallel. This objective had been accomplished by the end of September 1950 and US thinking began to lean toward dislodging the Communist leadership in the North. In moving down this path, the political leadership in Washington was sensitive to minimising any risk of provoking intervention by the Soviet Union in particular, but also by China.

The charismatic US military commander in Korea, General Douglas MacArthur, was somewhat dismissive of these concerns and secured Washington's conditional approval to press north of the 38th parallel (shortly afterwards he was famously relieved of his command by direct Presidential order for insubordination). Confirmation that the US-led forces were not going to stop at the de facto border pushed Mao to allow Chinese forces to infiltrate undetected across the Yalu River in October and November and to counter-attack on 26 November 1950. To soften the move at least slightly, they were labelled 'volunteers', not regular formations of the People's Liberation Army (PLA), even though they numbered an estimated 200 000 men. Within a few weeks, Mao also succumbed to the temptation of complete victory and pursued coalition forces deep into the South.

The US decision to intervene surprised everyone but itself. The United States had envisaged prolonged instability on the peninsula, but concluded that its interests did not require being around to ensure a particular outcome. North Korea's invasion, seen as blatant and unprovoked, fell outside the terms of this assessment. The United States chose to regard the invasion as a direct challenge to the sanctity of internationally-agreed boundaries and thus a precedent that, if allowed to stand, could return to haunt it in arenas of greater strategic significance. The outbreak of war on the Korean Peninsula also provided the political impetus to endorse NSC-68, which became the initial blueprint for an urgent rearmament program. Thereafter, a military program that consumed 6–7 per cent of Gross Domestic Product (GDP), roughly double the figure experienced in the years between the two World Wars, became the norm in the United States.

In addition to deciding promptly to resist the invasion, the United States quickly determined that military action across the Taiwan Strait, whether instigated by Taiwan or China, could complicate the prosecution of the campaign in Korea. Additionally, the Sino-Soviet security pact presumably changed US thinking about being indifferent to Beijing completing its defeat of the Nationalists by invading Taiwan. On the second day of the Korean War, 26 June 1950, US President Harry S. Truman ordered the US 7th Fleet to patrol the Taiwan Strait so as to deter action by either party. For Mao, already predisposed to regard the United States as an enemy and relatively bereft of good intelligence or diplomatic reporting, the combination of US forces back on the Korean Peninsula and, it seemed, protecting its erstwhile allies on Taiwan, must have looked awfully like precursors to an attempt to reverse his take-over, and contributed to his decision to enter the war in Korea.

Another fallout from the Korean War is likely to have been confirmation for the Chinese that the Soviet Union was a calculating friend, not one to rely on in difficult circumstances. Stalin had provided the initial approval of the invasion, donated the necessary offensive weaponry, and assigned senior officers to help plan the campaign, but then stepped away. Given his misgivings about Mao, Stalin may have wanted to test Mao's commitment to Socialism and, indirectly, his loyalty to Moscow. Mao passed the test and, by becoming an enemy of the United States, deepened China's dependence on the Soviet Union. Taking a longer-term perspective, with China becoming disillusioned with the alliance so soon after it was created, and picking up considerable kudos in the Third World for standing up to the United States, the test probably backfired on Stalin and the Soviet Union. Similarly, the lesson Zhou Enlai took away from the Korean War was that China should never again allow itself to be used as a pawn by the Soviet Union.[2]

Further confirmation came in Sino-Soviet negotiations in 1950 on borders and spheres of influence. Stalin had abandoned his protectiveness of the deal struck at Yalta with the United States and agreed that China and the Soviet Union, as new strategic partners, should strike a new deal. Mao secured a sunset clause on Soviet privileges in Manchuria and acceptance of Chinese control in Xinjiang. But Outer Mongolia, the homelands of the Western Xionguu which the Ming succeeded in bringing into the empire in the late seventeenth century, was lost. Moscow had created (and dominated) a new Mongolian republic and made clear that the new state (which had been recognised by the short-lived Nationalist government of China) was non-negotiable. As noted earlier, after the Second World War, Britain ceased to press its interests in Tibet and China's sovereignty over this territory went uncontested.

---

2   Han Suyin, *Eldest Son: Zhou Enlai and the Making of Modern China 1989-1976*, Kodansha, New York, 1994, p. 232.

After the Korean War, China had set about rebuilding its international relationships, concentrating on the large middle ground between the two superpowers, or the states of what was to become the non-aligned movement. In the late 1950s, China drifted toward characterising the superpowers as co-hegemonists and intensified its efforts to be a third force at the head of the non-aligned movement. Zhou Enlai had established a strong rapport with India's Prime Minister, Jawaharlal Nehru, in 1954–55, and played a prominent role at the famous non-aligned conference in Bandung, Indonesia in 1955, including the development and adoption of the Five Principles of Peaceful Coexistence. At this time, China also secured (at Soviet insistence, which it probably provided because Washington was adamantly opposed to the idea) a seat at the Geneva Conference convened to find an enduring settlement to the Korean War and to try to stop the increasingly complex conflict in Vietnam. Zhou evidently viewed China's participation as a coming-out event, renting a large villa on the outskirts of Geneva and turning up with a delegation of 150.

These gains were to be short-lived. Over the course of the 1950s, with China in a poisonous non-relationship with the United States, the alliance with the Soviet Union remained somewhat tepid as the two Socialist giants tried, without success, to define the basis for an enduring partnership. Specifics aside, Moscow's strong disposition to require clear recognition and acceptance of its leadership of the Socialist camp clashed with Beijing's hyper-sensitivity to subordinate status. The two countries clashed over Soviet Premier Nikita Khrushchev's wholesale trashing of Stalin's legacy. While China may have suspected that Stalin had manipulated them into confronting the United States in Korea, it had also embraced some of the core socialist ideas on economic development that he held dear, not least the collectivisation of agriculture. Similarly, Beijing queried Moscow's right to take corrective action in Poland and Hungary without consultation. Soviet-Chinese sparring over ideology became a dominant fixture of the periodic meetings of Socialist leaders, not least over Vladimir Lenin's conviction that war with the capitalist world was inevitable. The Soviet leadership had begun to distance itself from this tenet, while Mao remained a devotee, including to the corollary that Socialism needed to give first priority to ensuring that it would prevail in this war.

Zhou Enlai's early instincts that the United States would be a far more rewarding economic partner for China than the Soviet Union were confirmed. Moscow was exceedingly careful with its economic and technical assistance, and inclined to exploit, as fully as possible, the dependencies this assistance generated. This became particularly clear in the nuclear field where Moscow had agreed to assist China in developing its own nuclear weapon, but became progressively more reluctant to transfer critical technologies and knowhow. When it was acknowledged at the leadership level in 1958–59 that the differences were irreconcilable, and the Soviet Union abruptly terminated all of its assistance programs, China had been expecting a promised warhead design for some two years.

By the late 1950s, China had split with the Soviet Union and therefore had an antagonistic relationship with both superpowers. Moreover, China's rapport with India was frayed by skirmishes along the Tibet-India border in 1958–59 and India's agreement in March 1959 to provide political refuge for the Dalai Lama. In 1962, these tensions erupted into a full-scale border clash in which the PLA trounced the Indian Army and opened up a territorial dispute that remains unresolved today. India responded by qualifying its non-alignment and tilting toward the Soviet Union, although this tilt only became conspicuous after the 1971 Indo-Pakistani War and Indian perceptions that US naval deployments in the Bay of Bengal reflected an antagonistic stance toward New Delhi. (India was thereafter depicted in pink on Western political maps.) India also resolved in 1964, when China conducted its first nuclear test, to acquire a matching capability. China in turn, developed a close relationship with Pakistan and ultimately played a decisive role in that country's ability also to acquire a nuclear weapon capability by the late 1980s—a policy setting that kept India wholly pre-occupied with its Muslim neighbour and effectively locked-up on the sub-continent.

At the same time, China's modest momentum as a re-emergent player on the international stage was interrupted by the first of Mao's endeavours to recapture revolutionary fervour and, in this instance, channel it to achieve instant economic growth. The Great Leap Forward of 1958–59 attempted to tap into China's vast rural workforce and get them to also engage in village-level industrial production and infrastructure projects. Politically, the goal was to reconnect the leadership and the 'masses', bypassing the increasingly bureaucratised party machine that Mao sensed was marginalising him. An estimated 25–30 million peasants may have died of malnutrition as a result, and the economic disruption, combined with the withdrawal of Soviet technical assistance in 1959, produced several years of absolute decline in China's GDP.[3]

In the early 1960s, the flimsy understandings on Vietnam reached at the Geneva conference in 1955 began to fall apart and US involvement began to escalate. Both Beijing and Moscow desired to be Hanoi's primary partner, although neither wanted to be seen as actively frustrating the other's assistance. China had to endure the shipment of Soviet supplies to Hanoi through China, although it insisted on having full control while this material was on Chinese territory; that is, no Soviet personnel were permitted on Chinese soil to manage, facilitate

---

3   John K. Fairbank and Edwin O. Reischauer, *China: Tradition and Transformation*, Allen & Unwin, Sydney, 1989, pp. 396–99.

or oversee these shipments. The volume of Soviet aid quickly exceeded that from China, although the latter would stress that all its aid was unconditional: no repayment was sought or expected.

China's long and bitter history with Vietnam also echoed into the 1960s. China stressed that it supported Vietnamese nationalism and reunification, but would not countenance Vietnamese hegemony over Cambodia and Laos. This shadow over Beijing's support for North Vietnam's President Ho Chi Minh had developed back in the 1930s when Ho renamed his movement the Communist Party of Indochina. The strength of this lingering aversion to anything resembling a competing centre of power in China's immediate region became apparent when Hanoi, presumably with some measure of concurrence from Moscow, ignored Chinese sensitivities and invaded Cambodia in 1977, deposing Pol Pot and the ruling political party, the Khmer Rouge. In a very traditional fashion, Beijing determined that its authority in the region mandated a sharp military strike to teach the Vietnamese a 'lesson'. The PLA strike was indeed sharp and short although, by all accounts, and as had been the case so often in Vietnam over the centuries, the Chinese forces only narrowly avoided actual defeat.

As the intensity of the war in Vietnam escalated, China threw itself into another ideological convulsion—the Cultural Revolution (1966–76)—designed to preserve Mao's position from opponents with power bases within the Party, again with devastating consequences for China's economic wellbeing and for the coherence of its foreign policy.

US-China re-engagement

Ironically, just when China's leaders were indulging their whims and paranoia with little regard to the consequences for the general public, the United States began to test the waters for the resumption of normal relations and, perhaps something a little stronger. It had taken several years for the Sino-Soviet split in 1959–60 to be accepted by policymakers in the West as deep and irrevocable and something that could be reliably factored into strategic assessments. And it took several more years, probably until North Vietnam's Tet Offensive in 1968, for the United States to begin to lose confidence in its capacity to defeat the North or hold the South in Vietnam at a cost acceptable to the US Congress and the American public. The immediate motive for the overture to China was to create a stronger constellation of forces to construct a basis for a face-saving US withdrawal from Vietnam. The longer-term motive, dependent on securing something stronger than 'normal' relations with China, was to tilt the global balance in the Cold War further against the Soviet Union. Despite the huge distractions of the Cultural Revolution, Beijing was not about to reject so historic an invitation. The most powerful nation in the world, one that the new China had stumbled into war with in 1950–53, that was making powerful again China's most mortal enemy of recent times (Japan), and one that had refused even to shake a Chinese hand at the Geneva Conference on Indochina in 1955, was seeking China's friendship.

Developments with the Soviet Union also made better relations with the United States look attractive and most timely. China's leaders took the possibility of superpower collusion against them quite seriously. Beijing was concerned about Moscow's forceful intervention in Czechoslovakia in 1968 and the articulation of the so-called Brezhnev Doctrine by which Moscow reserved the right to use force to deal with errant behaviour in the Socialist camp. Then, from March 1969, Chinese and Soviet forces clashed in a series of border skirmishes along the Ussuri River, some quite significant in scale, and US intelligence reported evidence of a more wide-ranging build-up of Soviet nuclear and conventional forces in the Far East.

The story of US-China re-engagement from 1971–72 is broadly known.[4] The two sides struck a practical bargain that developed over the next 20 years into something that had more depth and diversity to it than was readily apparent. China clearly relished getting back into the major league, but was equally determined to be cautious and principled in laying the foundations of its relationship with the United States, and even more determined to not convey the slightest hint of gratitude or indebtedness to Washington. It can be safely presumed that Beijing wanted to convey the impression that dealing with the great and powerful as equals represented normality for China.

Like the United States in respect of generating better conditions for an honourable exit from Vietnam, China's specific hope was that re-engaging with the United States might unlock Taiwan. Neither side could, nor wished to, accommodate fully the other's immediate aim. China insisted that the re-unification of Vietnam was a just cause and refused to pressure Hanoi to qualify its war aims. Yet, it did address a concern that had nagged the United States for years; namely that, as in Korea, Chinese forces might intervene alongside those of North Vietnam: China said this would not happen, so long as it was clear, of course, that the United States had no designs on China itself. China did rather better on the subject of Taiwan. In the Shanghai Communiqué of February 1972, the United States accepted the one-China principle; no support for Taiwanese independence; no encouragement of closer Japanese involvement

---

4   One of the best accounts can be found in James Mann, *About Face: A History of America's Curious Relationship with China, from Nixon to Clinton,* Alfred A. Knopf, New York, 1999.

in Taiwan and, of course, China taking over Taiwan's seat at the United Nations, including permanent membership on the UNSC. But Taiwan was not 'unlocked' and continues to bedevil bilateral relations today.

On the broader target of the opening to China—the Soviet Union—it was easier to find common ground. The United States promptly began to share some of its intelligence on the disposition of Soviet forces in China's vicinity. By 1975–76, again at US initiative, this had developed into proposals for regular, institutionalised intelligence exchanges and for the provision of military assistance. In 1979, China agreed to host US signals intelligence facilities to monitor Soviet missiles tests—a function that the United States had performed from facilities in Iran until the Islamic revolution of that year. In the early 1980s, in addition to removing China as a primary strategic nuclear target in the Single Integrated Operational Plan (SIOP), the Reagan Administration went so far as to direct the Pentagon to plan for the provision of security assistance to China in the event of Soviet aggression.[5]

Washington also tried to reassure Beijing that it had nothing to fear from US-Soviet détente. One strand of Chinese difficulty with Khrushchev had been concern that his interest in more stable relations with the United States would be a prelude to superpower collusion against China. After 1971–72, Beijing shifted this concern to Washington. Beijing linked the alleviation of this concern strongly to the full normalisation of bilateral relations with the United States, a Richard Nixon/Henry Kissinger promise that was repeatedly delayed by domestic political developments like the Watergate scandal and the rise of the right wing of the US Republican Party. When it eventually occurred in 1979, under President Jimmy Carter, it was accompanied by the *Taiwan Relations Act* which went about as far as Congress could go toward replacing the security commitment that the United States had given Taiwan when it was recognised as the government of China, including helping Taiwan to maintain a 'sufficient self-defence capability'.

The importance of China and how important the Chinese should be encouraged to think they were to the United States during the Cold War was a hotly contested issue in Washington. Over the seven years or so that passed between the opening to China in 1972 and the normalisation of bilateral relations in 1979 an enduring split on this issue developed in the US policy community. The debate in Washington pivoted on the question of who had the most to gain from the relationship and, therefore, who should be regarded as courting whom? Those who pressed for playing close attention to the development of

---

5   Hans M. Kristensen, Robert S. Norris, Matthew G. McKinsie, *Chinese Nuclear Forces and US Nuclear War Planning,* The Federation of American Scientists, and The Natural Resources Defense Council, November 2006, p. 153, available at <http://www.nukestrat.com/china/chinareport.htm>, accessed 24 June 2009.

the relationship based their argument, fundamentally, on the decisive value of China's Western inclination to the Cold War strategy of containing the Soviet Union. And it was the case that, from the mid 1960s onwards, the Soviet Union deployed substantial conventional and nuclear forces in its far eastern territories, adding significantly to what turned out to be an unsustainable military effort. This assessment inclined successive administrations to deal with human rights issues in China with the greatest discretion; to officially encourage European suppliers of defence and defence-related items to provide what China wanted but the United States could not supply; to offer (in January 1980) to sell advanced 'non-lethal' defence-related technologies; to grant China Most Favoured Nation (MFN) status in 1979, effectively giving China the same access to US markets as most other states in the world; and to tolerate relentless Chinese pressure to more completely sever its ties with Taiwan.

The high-water mark of this assessment of China's importance was the August 1982 US-China Communiqué agreeing to restraints on military sales to Taiwan. Thereafter, with both US President Ronald Reagan and US Secretary of State George P. Shultz persuaded that the United States had been too eager, the domestic balance of power on China shifted against ascribing primary importance to this relationship and, specifically, against the corollary of 'abandoning' Taiwan.

Nevertheless, within the parameters already laid down, the relationship continued to broaden, not least in terms of large-scale supplies of Chinese weapons to the Mujahideen in Afghanistan, financed by the Central Intelligence Agency, and in terms of Chinese defence purchases from the United States. As we shall see, however, there were also accumulating signs of China's preparedness to signal that it did not feel 'dependent' on the United States for protection from the Soviet Union and was quite prepared to cut across US interests if they clashed with its own.

In addition, the China that the United States had engaged with in 1972 began an internal transformation in 1978 that was to have global ramifications. In that year, China's supreme leader, Deng Xiaoping, led the country away from socialist techniques for resource allocation and embraced the market economy internally and externally. Barely two years after the death of Mao, Deng succeeded in committing China to the development of a market economy and to opening China up to the international economic system. This represented a bold strategic judgement that China had to go back to basics and to restore the fundamental basis of power in any state, that is, its economic strength.

Deng, it could be said, had a 'grand strategy' to drive China back into a respectable position among the world's major states through a deliberate and methodical process of focusing the nation's energy on successive stepping stones. A word on grand strategy may be in order. It does not mean doctrine or any kind of thematic strategy like a political, economic or defence strategy. All of these are more specific or concrete endeavours to organise means to achieve defined ends. Grand strategy involves the broadest or most elemental judgements about the forces at work in the world, particularly the primary agents of change, and determining which broad direction or setting for the nation's capacities is most advantageous and to which all more specific strategies must contribute or at least not contradict. The open-ocean yachtsman may provide a useful analogy. He or she must decide whether the best winds are to be found well out to sea or closer to the coast. If the wrong judgement is made, then even the most skilful seamanship (in itself a complex of strategies and tactics) is likely to prove futile. Similarly, even if the right judgement is made, that complex of more specific strategies and tactics which constitute good seamanship will still be necessary to make good use of the success at the level of grand strategy. Grand strategy, in other words,

> refers to the central logic that informs and links [a state's foreign, economic and security policies], the regime's vision about how it can most sensibly serve the nation's interests (goals) in light of the countries capabilities (means) and the international constraints it faces (the context of interdependent choice).[6]

It would be difficult to underestimate the magnitude of the political task Deng undertook to 'sell' his grand strategy. First, he had to persuade China's Communist political leadership that socialist techniques for the production and distribution of wealth were conspicuously inferior to those of the market economy. It seems reasonable to suppose that Deng drew on the fact that China had tried the socialist way for three decades, but was still being outclassed to the point of humiliation by its mortal enemy of recent times (Japan), by its errant province (Taiwan) and by other entities like South Korea that had for millennia looked to China as an aspirational benchmark. After the fall of the Soviet Union, Francis Fukuyama was to call the triumph of the liberal democracy/market economy model 'the end of history', or the end of a centuries-long quest for the optimal combination of principles for the design of the nation-state. Fifteen years earlier, however, Deng had cast off one half of the socialist model (the economic half) in 1978 with a simple homile: 'It does not matter whether a cat is black or white so long as it catches mice.'

To sell his case, Deng also argued that the superpowers were in a robust stalemate and that 'peace and development' would increasingly become the dominant strands of national endeavour. Moreover, China was well positioned between the superpowers. China's cautious and practical but essentially 'normal' relationship

---

6   Avery Goldstein, *Rising to the Challenge: China's Grand Strategy and International Security*, Stanford University Press, Stanford, 2005, p. 19.

with the United States contrasted sharply with its 'hostile' relations with the Soviet Union and had a useful deterrent effect on the latter. Taken together, Deng was able to convince the various elements of the leadership community that what he proposed was a necessary but judicious gamble. As we shall see below, Deng even managed to cut a deal with the PLA to contribute to the priority goal of accelerated economic growth by allowing its onerous share of central government resources, and of GDP, to fall sharply for a time.

Deng's grand strategy also broke with a tradition of controlled and limited entanglement with other countries that had endured for millennia. The only departure from this tradition, the largely involuntary entanglement with the industrialised European states plus the United States and Japan in the period 1850–1950, seemed only to underscore its essential wisdom.

The Chinese leadership recognised that Deng's prescription would involve China becoming progressively more interdependent with other states and involved risk in that its full consequences over the longer term, not least on the domestic political front, were impossible to anticipate with any certainty. Clearly, however, the assessment was that a commitment to the market economy, international trade, foreign investment and economic interdependence was so critical to the restoration of China's economic strength in a reasonable timeframe that such risks simply had to be accepted and managed as they appeared.

Until his death in 1997, Deng continued to urge the strongest possible focus on economic growth and development and holding in check other national aspirations until the strength of this foundation was no longer in doubt. His adages, including 'Hide our capacities and bide our time' and 'Be good at keeping a low profile' remained beacons for the Chinese elite for years after his death, even as it began to dawn that they were counter-productive in implying so strongly that China could have a different and less attractive agenda for the era beyond the restoration of its economic fortunes.

Deng's core thesis that peace between the major powers and a preoccupation with developing economic strength would be the defining features of the contemporary era, providing China with a window of opportunity to give maximum priority to its economic agenda without being unduly concerned that its basic security or wider geopolitical interests would be irredeemably eroded while it was thus preoccupied, proved remarkably durable. Events like the internal dissent in Tiananmen Square in June 1989, the collapse of the Soviet Union in 1989–91 (which challenged all governments that based their legitimacy on constructing a socialist society), the emergence of the United States as the unipolar power, and of the neo-conservative thinking on how it should utilise this position all provoked introspection about the basic wisdom of the course China was travelling. Thus far, however, China's leadership has elected to stay the course, to adjust its foreign and security policies in the light of changing circumstances so as to keep the window of opportunity open and to enable a continued focus on economic development.

Inevitably, perhaps, and not unforeseen, the encouragement of free enterprise and the accumulation of wealth, and of engagement with the predominately capitalist outside world, generated appetites for other freedoms and a propensity to test the system's inclination to grant them. From the mid 1980s, protest movements (focused variously on price rises, corruption, Japan and, at least indirectly, on political liberalisation) exhibited a significant potential to catch on, to grow in scale in one location and to spread quickly to others. It would seem that the United States essentially missed the significance of these signals. In the case of the Soviet Union, the United States was keenly interested in all manifestations of unrest and the methods Moscow used to squash them, both for their propaganda value and for what they might say about the Soviet Union's capacity to sustain the Cold War. The US perspective on China was very different: it was simply not in the business of making life difficult for the Chinese leadership and thus was prone to casual assessment of these episodes as inevitable turbulence in a basically positive process of transformation and reform.[7]

A second consequence of harnessing capitalist mechanisms to the economic side of the Socialist equation, that had a marked impact on the character of the Sino-American relationship, was international arms sales. Zhou Enlai used to boast that China neither sought nor expected compensation for the military assistance it provided. In the early 1980s, however, in addition to payments from the Central Intelligence Agency for arms supplied to the Afghan Mujahideen, China tapped into the bonanza provided by the Iraq-Iran war. Although China, for the most part, filled a substantial niche in the market for robust, low-cost weaponry and equipment, its missile sales progressively exposed the reality of a state with its own interests and, despite the informal anti-Soviet alliance, little inclination to be sensitive to US concerns.[8]

China's arms sales to Iran included a land-based anti-shipping missile code-named *Seersucker*. While a somewhat cumbersome system embodying old technology (its pedigree extends back to the *Silkworm* missile, the initial

---

7   See Mann, *About Face: A History of America's Curious Relationship with China, from Nixon to Clinton,* especially pp. 155–66.

8   Around this time (1982), China and the United Kingdom were negotiating the transfer of sovereignty over Hong Kong. Deng Xiaoping sought to underline the pro forma nature of these negotiations by telling the British Prime Minister (Margaret Thatcher) that he had the option of simply taking the colony 'this afternoon'. A senior Chinese official revealed subsequently that this was not simply a negotiating ploy: the People's Liberation Army had been readied to invade because it was feared that the announcement of a date for the handover would trigger anti-China unrest. See Michael Sheridan, 'China plotted Hong Kong invasion', *Australian,* 25 June 2007.

Chinese version of the *Styx*, a Soviet system from the 1950s), the *Seersucker* has a range of 100 km and a formidable 500 kg warhead. In the confines of the Persian Gulf and the Strait of Hormuz, the weapon was a genuine headache for the Pentagon.[9] China initially responded to US complaints in 1987 with outright denials of involvement in these transactions. It eventually gave an undertaking not to supply these missiles to Iran, while at the same time discreetly assisting Iran in building the capacity to manufacture the missile indigenously.

An even ruder shock came in early 1988 when the United States learned that China had already transferred 36 CSS-2 intermediate-range (2700 km) ballistic missiles to Saudi Arabia. In PLA service, the CSS-2 was a nuclear weapon delivery system. The Saudi version had been modified to carry a conventional warhead, but the United States was still furious that the two 'allies' had conspired in complete secrecy to introduce a capability that could provoke serious reactions and make US interests in the stability of the several military balances in the region (Arab-Israel, Arab-Persian, Iran-Iraq) so much harder to achieve.

Finally, in the late 1980s, with US intelligence alerted to the new challenge, the United States endeavoured to discourage China from proliferating its newer solid-fuelled tactical ballistic missiles, the M-9 (range 800 km, warhead 1000kg) and M-11 (range 300 km, warhead 500kg). The prospective markets of particular concern to the United States were Syria and Pakistan. What followed was a tortuous cat-and-mouse game extending well into the 1990s (and still the subject of much speculation) involving the transfer but not deployment of complete systems, the transfer of key components to be integrated into 'indigenous' missile development programs, repeated US sanctions on Chinese enterprises suspected of involvement in such transfers, and Beijing's exquisitely gradual commitment to comply fully with the guidelines of the Missile Technology Control Regime. This game allowed China to repeatedly set up opportunities to leverage its policy on missile exports for better conditions for trade and technology transfer, and, occasionally, for US concessions on Taiwan.

Some broader considerations may also have been at work, reinforcing China's propensity to be an increasingly 'rebellious' member of the anti-Soviet Union coalition. In the late 1960s and 1970s, China's immediate concerns about a military threat from the Soviet Union were reinforced by assessments that the

---

9   Both sides in the 1980–88 Iran-Iraq War attempted to damage the other's capacity to pump and transport oil, a tactic that produced friction with naval forces deployed to the Gulf to protect the security of oil supplies. In 1987–88, China's determined efforts to protect a positive relationship with Iran were made more difficult by Tehran's preparedness to threaten 'Western' and neutral shipping in the Strait of Hormuz with sea mines and Chinese land-based anti-ship Seersucker missiles. In October 1987, a missile struck a tanker being escorted by the US Navy, which retaliated by destroying an Iranian offshore oil production platform. In April 1988, a US frigate struck a mine, resulting in wider US retaliation. For a fuller discussion of these events, see John W. Garver, *China and Iran: Ancient partners in a Post-Imperial World*, University of Washington Press, Seattle, 2006, especially pp. 82–93.

correlation of forces globally had tilted in favour of the Soviet Union. These considerations encouraged a rather more conspicuous tilt toward the United States. In the 1980s, with the Soviet Union bleeding in Afghanistan and the United States embarked on a massive military buildup (including the Strategic Modernization Program (addressing offensive nuclear forces), the Strategic Defense Initiative (Star Wars) and the 600-ship navy), the pendulum swung the other way, inclining Beijing, if not to tilt towards the Soviet Union, at least to perceive greater safety in stepping out on its own road.[10] Additionally, of course, Beijing would not have missed the signals from Washington from 1982–83 that the propensity to woo China had weakened appreciably.

Post-Cold War: The United States repositions China in its worldview

There were, as we have just seen, a number of pointers to the fact that the US-China relationship in the latter half of the 1980s was beginning to break out of its original parameters—a pragmatic political accommodation with a hint of alliance to confront a common enemy in the Soviet Union. Then came the suppression of student protests in Tiananmen Square on 4 June 1989, an episode that transformed popular attitudes in the United States and around the world toward China. Business as usual with Beijing became politically untenable, particularly in the United States and the rest of the Western world. This sudden estrangement was soon compounded by a far more deep-seated watershed—the collapse of the Cold War order between November 1989 when the Berlin Wall came down and December 1991 when the Soviet Union disintegrated.

We speculated earlier in this paper about whether, and how strongly, the foreign and security policy drivers in imperial China echoed into the modern era. This question now began to intrigue American security analysts and to find expression in investigations into China's probable 'grand strategy'. Over the course of the 1990s, the need to rely on abstract judgements by professional Sinologists about China's likely 'grand strategy' diminished. The Chinese Government's penchant for secrecy remained pretty much intact, but China became a far more visible and active player on the international stage, providing a relative abundance of data points to be evaluated and linked as a basis for judgements about the thinking that informed Chinese policies.

---

10 See Ron Huisken, *America and China: A Long-Term Challenge for Statesmanship and Diplomacy*, SDSC Working Paper no. 386, Strategic and Defence Studies Centre, The Australian National University, Canberra, March 2004.

The end of the Cold War saw a surge of interest in the United States in China, its ambitions, and its capacity to realise those ambitions, especially as the suppression of student protests in June 1989 had shattered generally optimistic expectations of a political transformation as well as an economic one.

In retrospect, it would appear that, as the shadow of the Soviet Union faded from the scene, the United States formed the view that if the significant space on its 'radar screen' formerly occupied by the Soviet Union was to be filled in due course by another power, that power was most likely to be China. In the early 1990s, this prospect had none of the shape or perceived imminence needed for focused policy development, but it is likely that Washington and Beijing have been interacting with a shared sense of such a future since that time.

The end of the Cold War came as a considerable surprise to both policymakers and academics. Few had spent any time thinking about how to deal with this development. In Europe, however, being taken by surprise proved to be no handicap. With the North Atlantic Treaty Organization (NATO) and the European Union serving as critical safety nets, the old order cascaded into the new with astonishing speed. The Berlin Wall came down, Germany re-unified, the Warsaw Pact was dissolved and the 'iron curtain' raised, the Red Army went home, and home (the Soviet Union) broke up. All in the space of 25 months, and all without a shot being fired.

In East Asia, in stark contrast, it seemed that absolutely nothing happened. This was an illusion, of course. It was quickly appreciated that, in strategic terms, East Asia (and especially Northeast Asia) remained as the major piece of unfinished business from the Cold War and therefore a key determinant of the ultimate shape of the post-Cold War order. Relationships of power and influence were still underdeveloped and fluid. Moreover, it soon became apparent just how important the Soviet threat had been to sustaining relatively harmonious relations among the big three—the United States, China and Japan. Managing these relationships without the Soviet Union was to prove tantamount, in some respects, to going back to the beginning, to the pre-Cold War days. And there were not too many positives from those days to build on.[11]

As China and the United States began, more or less unconsciously, to test the parameters of their post-Cold War relationship, they discovered that the comparative harmony of the 1970s and 1980s had been lost. Though probably

---

11   These circumstances produced a spate of influential articles on the theme that East Asia retained more strongly than any other region the ingredients for war between the major powers. See, for example, Richard K. Betts, 'Wealth, Power and Instability: East Asia and the United States after the Cold War', *International Security*, vol. 18, no. 3, Winter 1993–94, pp. 34–77; and Aaron L. Friedberg, 'Ripe for Rivalry: Prospects for Peace in a Multipolar World', *International Security*, vol. 18, no. 3, Winter 1993–94, pp. 5–33.

hazy on both sides, their respective visions of the preferred relationship between them—and, by implication, the influence that each was prepared to concede to the other in shaping the future of Asia—were different, and diverging.

In retrospect, it may well have been the case at the outset of the post-Cold War era that China developed inflated expectations about the scope available to exploit the new fluidity on the international scene to position it more favourably in the regional hierarchy of power and influence. The factors contributing to such a frame of mind are not hard to discern. China had, after all, been a behind-the-scenes but rather close strategic partner of the United States for 20 years—closer in fact than many people realised because the relationship had comparatively little visibility.[12] Moreover, with its particular historical baggage, and all the hype about the power it was expected to become, the Chinese leadership may have felt encouraged to reap earlier rewards and be more assertive about the role it expected to play. Furthermore, in addition to the mainstream academic (and, indeed, governmental) prognosis for a relatively brisk transition to multipolarity, it would have seemed in Beijing that the United States was signalling that it intended to loosen its strategic grip on Asia and provide more space for other actors. US President George H.W. Bush was speaking of a 'new world order'; prosecuted the first Gulf War in strict compliance with UNSC resolutions which authorised the liberation of Kuwait, not unseating the regime in Baghdad; signalled a diminution of US military power to 'just enough' to protect US interests and meet US obligations; planned significant reductions in its forces forward-deployed in Europe and Northeast Asia; accepted the loss of its major air and naval bases in the Philippines in 1992; and was prepared to push its trade disputes with Japan to the point of jeopardising the political and even security dimensions of the relationship with this hitherto pivotal ally.

What China appears to have found difficult to fully appreciate was the extent to which the events in Tiananmen Square had transformed the generally positive impressions of China in the West, and China's abrupt demotion in strategic importance to the United States following the demise of the Soviet Union. In any event, as the United States gradually absorbed the full implications of winning the Cold War and began to develop new policy bearings for the still strangely fluid post-Cold War era, it looked upon China with very different eyes. Far from being regarded as the co-determinant of the future order in Asia, Beijing found itself regarded as a prospectively dangerous loose cannon lacking the disciplines of democracy, respect for human rights and compliance with the established norms and conventions of international conduct in fields like trade and non-proliferation.

---

12 See Mann, *About Face: A History of America's Curious Relationship with China, from Nixon to Clinton,* especially pp. 369–76.

The US-China relationship in the early 1990s began to be dominated by differences, above all Taiwan, human rights and proliferation, both nuclear and conventional. In addition, the United States changed course with Japan, restoring the primacy of the political and security relationship, froze the planned reductions in its forward-deployed forces, and reaffirmed its determination to resist the threat or use of force to secure the incorporation of Taiwan into China. The Clinton Administration ultimately settled firmly on a policy of engagement toward China, but the Republican-led debate in the United States on the alternative of containment was by no means just political posturing.

China has never been enamoured of the US alliances with Asian states, and the forward-deployed forces that attended these arrangements. During the Cold War, Beijing's official stance on alliances waxed and waned with its assessment of how the correlation of forces was tilting the East-West balance, and on where Beijing saw itself positioned in that balance at the time.[13] With the end of the Cold War, China initially took a relatively tolerant line: there was no particular urgency, but alliances were anachronistic hangovers from a bygone era that should have no place in the new one.

Ongoing friction with the United States eroded this tolerance until two developments apparently tipped the scales. The first was the confrontation with the United States over Taiwan in 1995–96, when China's attempt to weaken the appeal of pro-independence groups through missile tests provoked the United States to step away from its policy of 'strategic ambiguity' and to deploy two US carrier battle groups in waters near Taiwan. This was the first time since 1958 that either side had resorted to the coercive use of military forces to underscore their positions in respect of Taiwan.

The second was the Joint Declaration by the United States and Japan in April 1996 strongly re-affirming the relevance of their alliance into the indefinite future. As part of this declaration, Japan undertook to develop new defence guidelines to better define its military role within the alliance as well as the geographic area deemed to be within the scope of alliance operations. For Beijing, the one major benefit of the US-Japan alliance was that it obviated the need for Japan to provide fully for its own defence. In Beijing's eyes, it now seemed that the alliance was to become a springboard for Japan's 'normalisation' as a security actor and, in all probability, for further development of its military capabilities.

---

13   For additional observations on this issue, see Ron Huisken, 'Accelerating the Evolutionary Process of Security Cooperation in the Asia-Pacific: An Australian Perspective', in See Seng Tan and Amitav Acharya (eds), *Asia-Pacific Security Cooperation: National Interests and Regional Order*, M.E. Sharpe, Armonk, NY, 2004, pp. 38–42.

In 1996–97, it was widely reported that China had made the fundamental determination that, on balance, the direct and prominent US role in the security equation in East Asia was no longer in China's interests and that China should seek to weaken that role.[14] As we shall see, however, the question of how and when to pursue this objective became subordinate to the broader policy judgement that China needed to continue to give first priority to economic development. This, in turn, meant maintaining the most constructive possible relationships with the countries, especially the United States, whose markets, capital and technology remained critical to sustaining China's economic trajectory.

When US President George W. Bush assumed office in January 2001, his Administration essentially codified the preceding decade of difficulty and deterioration in US-China relations. During the election campaign, the Bush team had bluntly characterised China as a strategic competitor. Once in office, it consciously took a more detached or aloof approach to China, signalling— as befits a sole superpower—that China was an important concern but not especially important. In an early crisis—the collision between a Chinese fighter aircraft and a US intelligence-gathering EP-3 aircraft in international airspace off Hainan Island in April 2001—the Bush Administration conspicuously resisted elevating its significance and pursued a resolution through normal diplomatic channels. Moreover, with no particular subtlety, it flexed its muscles. In the delicate psychological game over Taiwan, it tilted conspicuously in favour of Taiwan, with Bush declaring that the United States would do 'whatever it takes' to help Taiwan defend itself. The Bush Administration followed this up in April 2001 with the most generous arms package for Taiwan since 1992. As a US Department of State official put it in 2002: 'Taiwan is not looked at as a problem anymore. We look at it as a success story.'[15] China clearly remained suspicious that US insistence on peaceful reunification was a cover for a more strategic objective, namely to protect Taiwan's considerable value as a military complication for China. In protesting the US decision to allow Taiwan's Defence Minister to attend a conference in Florida in March 2002, a Chinese Vice Foreign Minister exposed this view when he urged the United States to abandon its policy of regarding Taiwan as an 'unsinkable aircraft carrier'.[16]

In May 2001, the Bush Administration also accelerated and recast the missile defence program in ways that would have made it seem an even more serious prospective challenge to China's nuclear deterrent. In particular, the Administration erased the distinction between strategic or national and

14   See, for example, Jim Hoagland, 'China: Two Enquires…', *Washington Post,* 20 July 1997. The evidence for this policy shift has remained anecdotal.

15   Quoted in John Pomfret, 'In Fact and in Tone, US Expresses New Fondness for Taiwan', *Washington Post,* 30 April 2002.

16   Quoted in Bonnie S. Glasser, 'Two Steps Forward, One Step Back', *Comparative Connections,* (An E-Journal on East Asian Bilateral Relations), 16 April 2002.

theatre missile defence systems, insisting that advances in capability would be exploited wherever they occurred. This development was re-enforced by the US decision in December 2001 to withdraw unilaterally from the Anti-Ballistic Missile (ABM) Treaty (a decision that came into effect in June 2002), despite solemn joint warnings from China and Russia (not to mention many European Union countries) that this would weaken global stability. The United States was at pains to stress that it had no interest in or intent to degrade the nuclear deterrent of other established nuclear weapon states.[17] Still, it should be borne in mind that the US withdrawal from the ABM Treaty meant that Russia and China would have to rely solely on US *political* assurances that it would limit missile defences to the numerically small threat from 'rogue' states.

Finally, in its *Quadrennial Defence Review* (QDR) (released in October 2001) the Bush Administration announced far-reaching changes in policy and posture regarding US conventional forces.[18] Among other things, for the first time in decades the QDR made Asia the region of primary interest and concern—ahead of Europe and the Middle East. Within Asia, in contrast to the past focus on Korea, the QDR signalled US determination to put itself in a position through enhanced long-range strike capabilities and more readily deployable ground forces, so as to shape more closely the security environment across the region as a whole. The Pentagon called the new area of special interest the 'East Asian Littoral', defined as extending from south of Japan, through Australia and into the Bay of Bengal. The QDR made it abundantly clear that US objectives for this region were very much driven by caution about China; that is, the United States adopted a hedging strategy.

It is also very likely that China was conscious of the neoconservative strand in US strategic thinking that developed in the Pentagon in 1990–92 into the thesis that, with the demise of the Soviet Union, the United States had a historic opportunity, even a duty, to perpetuate unassailable superiority and to use it to project its (universal) values and beliefs across the globe. This thesis, leaked to the press in 1992, sparked a major controversy, and was emphatically rejected by then US President George H.W. Bush. Although its most senior champion, then Secretary of Defense Richard Cheney, succeeded in putting a softer version

---

17 The United States acknowledges a formal strategic nuclear relationship with Russia (as the successor to the Soviet Union), with their mutual interests and responsibilities codified in the Anti-Ballistic Missile (ABM) and SALT/START agreements. This includes, as a practical matter, recognising Russia's 'right' to be able to deter the United States through capacities to mount a nuclear strike. The United States has never recognised China in this way, and remains reluctant to grant China the kudos associated with doing so. Accordingly, while Washington was obligated to reassure Moscow about its strategic intentions (even though it was abrogating the treaty that most clearly articulated this obligation), this was no more than an option in respect of Beijing. Washington did exercise the option, but used then Secretary of State Colin Powell to deliver the assurances discreetly in the context of a regular visit to China.

18 See Ron Huisken,, *QDR 2001: America's New Military Roadmap*, SDSC Working Paper no. 366, Strategic and Defence Studies Centre, The Australian National University, Canberra, March 2002.

of this thesis on the public record just days before Bill Clinton was inaugurated in January 1993, this radical grand strategy vanished from the scene until it was spectacularly revived without debate by US President George W. Bush in June 2002. While Americans may have lost sight of this proposal for a new grand strategy for the United States, it is very likely that it remained in the back of the mind of Chinese policymakers and was a factor in their strategic deliberations.[19]

In 2000, Michael Swaine and Ashley Tellis published an influential assessment of China's grand strategy, together with a realist projection of how that strategy might evolve over the first half of the twenty-first century.[20] This analysis characterised China's traditional or imperial grand strategy as a trilogy of goals: (1) domestic order and well-being; (2) defence against external threats; and (3) geopolitical status and influence commensurate with being a major and, ideally, the primary state in its region. Surveying China's behaviour since the death of Mao and the winding down of the last of the ideological convulsions he inspired (the Cultural Revolution), Swaine and Tellis concluded that China had adopted a 'calculative' strategy—an awkward term, but one with considerable merit.

The label 'calculative' stems from the reasonable inference that China's leaders recognised that 30 years of using socialist tools and looking to others in the socialist bloc to rebuild China had accomplished little in the way of elevating China's relative status in the community of states, and that its profound weaknesses relative to other major powers would endure unless everything was subordinated to a revival of its economic strength.

During the period needed to rebuild its economic strength, China would have to continue to manage its non-economic ambitions, including its security interests, from a position of relative weakness. This involved keeping the number of objectives about which China was prepared to be assertive to an absolute minimum, and selecting them carefully so that China would not be caught out defining objectives that were beyond the product of its physical capacities and its political will at any point in time to protect and defend.

Swaine and Tellis then go on to offer a realist projection of how China's grand strategy can be expected to evolve over the course of the twenty-first century. As continued economic growth expands China's weight and influence, it will reach tipping-points relative to other actors (either individual states or collectives like the Association of Southeast Asian Nations (ASEAN)) where

---

19   For a more complete account of the genesis of this thesis, see Ron Huisken, 'Iraq: The Neocon Strategy', *Agenda*, December 2006. Although the Neocon thesis is strongly associated with the 11 September 2001 terrorist attacks on the United States and the invasion of Iraq, a strong case can be made that it informed the George W. Bush Administration's foreign and security policy thinking from the outset.

20   Michael D. Swaine and Ashley J. Tellis, *Interpreting China's Grand Strategy: Past, Present, and Future*, RAND Corporation, Santa Monica, 2000, available at <http://rand.org/pubs/monograph_reports/MR1121/>, accessed 24 June 2009.

their dependency on China exceeds their capacity to inhibit China's economic performance, liberating China's strategic calculations. Similarly, China's military capacity to deter, intimidate or defeat other powers in locations and scenarios Beijing considers important will expand, even though other powers would also be expanding their capabilities. These authors anticipated that China would experience the same pressures as rising powers in the past: accumulating an expanding set of international interests and obligations, seeking to elevate its standing in the international system, and seeing the ambitions of its leadership expand with perceptions of rising capacities to fulfill them. According to Swaine and Tellis, we should expect that China will gradually outgrow its calculative stage and adopt more assertive policy settings.

Swaine and Tellis wisely resist the temptation to be prescriptive. Rather, they note that the world in which China is seeking to re-establish itself as an adequately influential player is very different not only from the 'world' that imperial China dominated in the past, but also very different from the experiences of Spain, France, Britain, Germany and Japan from which the 'realist' school derives its key tenets. For one thing, if it is the case that states are driven by the 'anarchic' international system ceaselessly to accumulate power to preserve their security, the only logical endpoint today is to achieve global hegemony. Subsequent to the revolutions in transport and communication technologies, China is unlikely to wish or to be able to be content with major power status (or pre-eminence or hegemony) just in Asia. Similarly, if power ultimately resides in the capacity to coerce other states, the ultimate source of such power has transitioned from industrial capacity to information-intensive technologies. Whether and when China could achieve or even begin to compete seriously for primacy in this field is a far more problematic proposition than whether it will become, statistically, the largest economy in the world or when it will acquire an undisputable capacity to preclude US intervention in support of Taiwan. In addition, if the realists are correct, the competition for supremacy in the coming decades is likely to evolve in an unfamiliar environment of multiple mega-states (most of them nuclear armed)—the likes of India, Brazil and possibly a revived Russia along with the United States, the European Union and China. How the old rules might play out in such an environment is anyone's guess.

Another prominent analyst, Robert Sutter, writing five years after Swaine and Tellis, broadly endorses their thesis and is correspondingly sceptical that the comparative tranquility of US-China relations in recent years has a robust basis or provides a reliable platform for assessments about the future.[21] Sutter acknowledges that the transformation in China's policies since the mid 1990s (see below) has been significant and important—too important in fact to be casually labelled as tactical. Still, Sutter insists that there is no consensus on

---

21   Robert G. Sutter, *China's Rise in Asia,* Rowman & Littlefield, Lanham, MD, 2005.

how deeply rooted these changes are, and therefore no consensus on what they suggest for the future. Most particularly, Sutter contends that, since the end of the Cold War, China has attached such importance to the United States that China's approach to, and policies toward, the United States essentially shape its foreign and security policies generally. Consistent with the Swaine/ Tellis 'calculative' thesis, Sutter inclines to the view that China has thus far determined that it is not ready to overtly contest US leadership in Asia. Put another way, China's intent is to displace the United States as the primary actor in Asia, but circumstances have compelled China to blend in and work with the United States for an indefinite period.

China re-calibrates

The new Chinese leadership under Jiang Zemin took a number of years to evaluate the implications of the end of the Cold War and the demise of the Soviet Union, including the effects these events had on the thinking of the other major powers. In particular, the cumulative difficulties with the United States in the years immediately following the Cold War tested the extant grand strategy articulated by the last of China's paramount leaders, Deng Xiaoping.

Something of a consensus has emerged that, around 1995–96, Beijing undertook a thorough review of the broad policy settings put in place to implement Deng grand strategy, against the new external landscape. In summary, this review reaffirmed his core assessments and priorities, not least the continued primacy of economic development (albeit qualified, as we shall see, by the decision to also accelerate military expenditure), but settled on a very different philosophy to inform the development of policies intended to achieve the broad purposes of the 'grand strategy'.[22]

A key judgement in this stocktake was that China's extant policy settings (and the attitudes and assessments that supported these policies) seemed to be exacerbating perceptions that China's rise was a threatening phenomenon and therefore likely to provoke countervailing strategies in other countries. This, in turn, could complicate China's priority interest in rebuilding its 'comprehensive national power' on the foundation of economic strength. It would appear that Beijing became newly sensitive to how disturbing China's rise might look from the outside (literally, the power of projections), but also to how China's assertive stance on issues like Taiwan and its extravagant territorial claims in the South China Sea could be exacerbating these concerns.

In other words, it would appear that the leadership recognised that it had misread the tea leaves in the early years of the post-Cold War era and succumbed to

---

22   Goldstein, *Rising to the Challenge: China's Grand Strategy and International Security*, p. 12.

temptations to seek a premature 'early harvest' in respect of its ambitions in East Asia. A particularly important judgement that emerged from this policy review was that unipolarity and US hegemony would be a longer lasting phenomenon than it had seemed would be the case in the early 1990s. The US economy had revived strongly and the initial signals that Washington was looking to a softer and more distant style of international leadership had been reversed. In short, the United States was becoming accustomed to unipolarity rather than inclined to welcome a transition to multipolarity. Moreover, there seemed to be little prospect over the coming decades that other major powers would acquire the capability and have the will to decisively erode US supremacy. This was a crucial judgement. It pushed further into the future China's acquisition of adequate power relative to the United States to contemplate any fundamental strategic re-ordering favourable to China. Looked at another way, it prolonged the era in which China's fortunes depended heavily on positive relations with the United States. For one thing, US markets, capital and technology remained decisive to China economic trajectory. For another, in order to give effect to the strategy of giving maximum priority to economic development, it was imperative that China avoid generating the view in the United States that it was a prospective strategic challenger and provoking Washington into a dedicated effort to block the development of China's power and influence.

Subsequent developments allow the inference that two further policy settings emerged to support the key objective of preserving a basically positive relationship with the United States. First, China should aspire to dispel absolutely its reputation as a spoiler or loose cannon and present itself as a responsible participant in the international system. The second could be seen as a 'hedge' in the event of unmanageable difficulties with the United States; namely, capitalising on China's economic needs and capacities to develop its political position and make China an attractive or at least indispensable partner for a broad range of influential actors on the international stage. This would benefit China directly and make it more difficult and costly for the United States to take a contrary stance toward China.

A number of developments in the latter half of the 1990s probably tested China's resolve to persist with the core judgements underpinning its grand strategy. The thrust of events and developments seemed to be moving in the direction of closer US interest in Asia and sharper interaction with China. The steady consolidation and development of US pre-eminence—most spectacularly in the military field—throughout the decade also visibly strengthened the pressures and temptations in the United States to act unilaterally to achieve its objectives. From China's perspective, two developments in the late 1990s were seen as further graphic examples of US disdain for China's interests. First, North Korea's launch of a rudimentary three-stage missile in August 1998 tilted the political balance in Washington on missile defence decisively in favour of a commitment to deploy. Even the limited deployment envisaged to cope with numerically small threats from 'rogue' states like North Korea could readily be shown to have the theoretical capability to negate China's modest nuclear deterrent. In addition, the sea-based component of the layered missile defence capabilities envisioned by the Pentagon could be deployed to cover Taiwan. The fact that Japan committed itself to acquire an almost identical sea-based missile defence capability only intensified these concerns. More to the point, China found it hard to disguise its view that these possible outcomes in fact constituted the real motives behind the US and Japanese missile defence programs, with Pyongyang merely providing a convenient political cover.

Second, when China and Russia adamantly opposed military intervention against Serbia (over humanitarian concerns in Kosovo) in the UNSC, the United States went ahead, with NATO support, but without any form of UN authorisation. And it accomplished its objectives. For China, dispassionate assessment of this episode was made difficult by the bombing of the Chinese Embassy in Belgrade in 1999 and the deaths of three Embassy personnel. The United States insisted that this was a simple accident, arising from the failure of the Pentagon to maintain accurate records (that is, US planes had struck the assigned target but did not know that it was now the Chinese Embassy). Unsurprisingly, many Chinese remain less than fully persuaded that the United States did not intend this 'accident' as a political message. In any event, Chinese scholarly writings on the Kosovo affair suggest that, within Chinese leadership circles—with an eye to Taiwan, Tibet, and the separatist movement in Xinjiang—confidence that the United States could be relied upon to be a relatively benign hegemon (an important element of China's grand strategy) declined rather sharply.

Despite these potential challenges and risks, China stuck to its decision to give developing its comprehensive national power absolute priority, particularly through adopting more proactive and reassuring foreign and security policy settings to create as much time and space as possible for this priority to be pursued without giving rise to alarm and reactive policies on the part of others.[23]

If developments on the missile defence front, US defiance of the UNSC in respect of Kosovo, and the assertive unilateralism that characterised the early policies of the Bush Administration tested the thrust of Deng's 'grand strategy', other developments were supportive of its continuing validity. Two developments were of particular importance in persuading the leadership that Deng's path remained a judicious gamble. One of these was the 11 September 2001 terrorist attacks on the United States, which is discussed below.

---

23   For an insightful assessment of these developments, see Bates Gill, *Rising Star: China's New Security Diplomacy*, Brookings Institution Press, Washington, DC, 2007.

The other was that China's post-1996 resolve to be more pro-active in keeping a benign and low profile, to actively attenuate concerns about its accumulating power and to replace the old label of 'loose cannon' with 'partner' and 'team player', began to pay off handsomely by the early years of the new century. The enhancement of China's status, accentuated by a distinct contrary trend in respect of the United States, strengthened the hand of those in leadership circles who felt that China was on the right track and should resist pressures and temptations to contemplate significant changes to its 'grand strategy'.

The new thinking on how best to advance the broad objectives of the 'grand strategy', perhaps most clearly evident in respect of Southeast Asia, centred on embracing multilateralism. China's growing weight in the economies of Southeast Asia states ensured heightened sensitivity to Chinese interests. For example, by 2005, China accounted for 8 per cent of ASEAN exports. This was still well short of the United States, European Union and Japan, but the share of these partners had slipped in recent times while China's had risen from around 2 per cent just 15 years earlier.[24] In sharp contrast to the United States, the European Union and Japan, China emerged from the 1997–98 Asian economic crisis as helpful and responsible. China did little more than decline to devalue its currency, but the Western powers found themselves tagged as having exacerbated the crisis through being thoughtlessly and arrogantly pro-active with painful and inappropriate economic prescriptions for dealing with the crisis.

At the same time, China shed its ambivalence about multilateralism in favour of being pro-active in the ASEAN Regional Forum (ARF) and the ASEAN Plus Three (APT), while also being supportive and protective of ASEAN's role as the 'driver' of these processes. China agreed to a code of conduct to defuse tensions over rival claims in the South China Sea (although the code of conduct's main effect is to defer rather than resolve the issue), and signed ASEAN's Treaty of Amity and Cooperation. In 2003, China's leadership launched its 'peaceful rise' slogan to replace the less marketable phrases authored by Deng 25 years earlier, only to conclude a year later that 'peaceful development' was even more felicitous, perhaps because it was more timeless and thus less likely to promote musing about what might follow China's 'rise'.

In the security arena, China moved more warily, perhaps mindful that a number of ASEAN states had not that long ago dealt with Chinese-supported insurgents, that security was the long pole in America's engagement with the region, and that most regional states valued this engagement rather highly. China did encourage the APT to extend its agenda beyond trade into the non-traditional security field but, both in the APT and the ARF, it has been noticeably more

---

24   Data on ASEAN trade and investment is taken from the ASEAN Secretariat website at <http://www. aseansec.org/13100.htm>, accessed 24 June 2009.

cautious than in the Shanghai Cooperation Organisation (SCO), where it is in the driver's seat. China has felt on safer ground in discreetly but relentlessly portraying its New Security Concept as more suited to the post-Cold War environment and more compatible with ASEAN values than the US alliance-based system (usually characterised euphemistically in Chinese commentary as the system based on a 'Cold War mentality'). To support this message, the PLA even initiated some substantively trivial but still unprecedented and therefore interesting transparency measures, and intensified the frequency of bilateral military-to-military contacts, naval visits and modest joint exercises. Even so, China stepped beyond ASEAN's comfort zone in 2004 by seeking a role in policing the Malacca Strait.

With the conspicuous exception of Myanmar—which is just as conspicuously outside the ASEAN mainstream—China has been very shy about arms sales, waiting to be asked rather than being pro-active. There has been a modest ice-breaking transaction with Thailand and a potentially more comprehensive arrangement with Indonesia involving short-range missiles and technical assistance to Indonesian defence industries.[25]

In short, although the speed of China's entrenchment in Southeast Asia and elsewhere has tended to produce exaggerated assessments of a fundamental shift in the balance of power that has already occurred, it seems undeniable that, in Southeast Asia in particular, Beijing is already well-positioned relative to the United States and Japan to compete for influence.

The 11 September 2001 terrorist attacks

The salience of Deng's grand strategy was reinforced indirectly by the fallout from the 11 September 2001 terrorist attacks on the United States. China was among the many states that spontaneously aligned themselves with the United States in the largest 'coalition of the willing' yet seen to signal that arbitrary violence of this kind could not be tolerated. Practical collaboration on terrorism was facilitated by US preparedness to list Islamic separatists in Xinjiang as terrorists. China subsequently became sceptical about and/or contested a number of dimensions of the US response to the terrorist attacks, notably the Pentagon's swift penetration of Central Asia and the drive against Iraq in the absence of a substantive link between that country and the events of 11 September 2001. In 2005, for example, the communiqué from the summit meeting of the SCO called on the United States to indicate when its forces would leave central Asia. While this call was not repeated in 2006 or 2007, it was a clear assertion by China and Russia of a priority claim to this region as their legitimate sphere of influence.

---

25 For a fuller account, see Carlyle A. Thayer, 'China's International Security Cooperation with Southeast Asia', *Australian Defence Force Journal*, no. 172, 2007.

From a broader perspective, however, the events of 11 September 2001 delivered an overwhelming benefit for China. It put on hold for an indefinite period the declared intent of the United States, for the first time in decades, to put Asia (and therefore China) ahead of Europe and the Middle East as the region of priority interest and concern for US foreign and security policy. Washington's diversion into the 'war on terror', and then its fateful decision to invade Iraq, will have reinforced Beijing's confidence that it could remain focused on building its economic power and political influence without attracting focused countervailing stratagems from Washington. The attractiveness of this prospect can be inferred from the fact that, as early as October 2002, China's President Jiang Zemin stepped away from France and Russia and told Bush privately that China would not use its veto in the UNSC to deprive the United States of a resolution 'authorising' the invasion of Iraq.

Taiwan and Korea: continuing flashpoints?

Taiwan

Taiwan can be said to be one of those accidents of history that harden into an issue that makes history. It is widely believed that neither China nor the United States believe that Taiwan is worth a war between them, but it has remained for decades the pre-eminent 'flashpoint' in the region.

For the People's Republic of China, emerging from the so-called 'century of humiliation' that straddled the demise of the imperial system, being fiercely defensive of its sovereignty lay at the core of its determination to 'stand up' and conduct its affairs free of coercion. We have seen how circumstances (dominated by the United States) conspired to allow China to retain nearly all of the empire that its imperial predecessors had regained in the preceding 400 years or so, leaving Chinese nationalist emotions focused on three relatively small blemishes: Hong Kong, Macau and Taiwan. Taiwan quickly emerged as the priority. Not only had significant Nationalist forces taken refuge on the island following their defeat in the civil war, Taiwan had been ceded to Japan in 1894 as part of a peace settlement following imperial China's defeat in the Sino-Japanese war of that year.

We have also seen that, despite Washington's disappointment with the defeat of its Nationalist Chinese allies during the war against Japan, the United States did not dispute China's claim to sovereignty over Taiwan and was reconciled to mainland forces invading the island and completing the victory, both over their internal opponents and, in some sense, over the Japanese. The Korean War radically altered the strategic calculus in Washington. On 26 June 1950, the day after North Korea invaded the South, US President Harry S. Truman ordered the US 7th Fleet to patrol the Taiwan Strait.[26] This was months before Chinese forces intervened so decisively in Korea, and Washington's public rationale was that it wished to preclude those on either side of the Taiwan Strait from actions that could complicate the challenge the United States faced in Korea. In fact, of course, China had aligned itself with the Soviet Union, including via a mutual security agreement, making it part of the Soviet bloc that the United States now recognised as its opponent in a pervasive 'cold war' and as the entity abetting North Korean aggression.

Washington's de facto and tangential commitment to the security of Taiwan naturally hardened after November 1950 when the war in Korea transitioned into a conflict essentially between US and Chinese forces—a conflict that the United States came perilously close to losing, and which led the United States to allude openly to its nuclear option. In the context of major power political and security calculations, and especially so in an environment of a global strategic contest, even de facto commitments assume great significance and are very difficult to undo. Policymakers worry that not living up to a commitment may embolden the opponent, possibly in arenas of greater strategic importance. They also worry that such actions will make allies less certain about the choice they have made, and neutral players more reluctant to make the 'right' choice. Washington's gravitation into Taiwan's security guarantor intensified in the 1950s. A major crisis erupted over the months of August 1954–May 1955 against the backdrop of US-Taiwanese consideration of a mutual security agreement, naturally seen in Beijing as a frontal assault of its sovereignty. The crisis involved artillery exchanges and air strikes from and against two islands (Quemoy and Matsu) that are technically Taiwanese, but which lie just a few kilometres off the coast of China. The United States was ambivalent about formally committing itself to the defence of these vulnerable Taiwanese territories, and the crisis was laced with public hints that, in the event the United States made such a commitment, the Pentagon advocated the use of tactical nuclear weapons to negate the rear-echelon capabilities that China would be able to bring to bear.

In the event, China and the United States, who had no diplomatic relations and therefore constrained communications, agreed to ambassadorial level talks as a means of defusing the crisis. The US-Taiwan security agreement was signed in November 1954. The agreement did not directly specify that the forward territories were included, and it contained language that gave the United States an effective veto over any attack by Taiwan on the Chinese mainland, but

---

26   For a fuller discussion on the management of US-China relations during the Korean War and the later crises over Taiwan, see Michael D. Swaine, Zhang Tuosheng and Danielle F.S. Cohen (eds), *Managing Sino-American Crises: Case Studies and Analysis,* Carnegie Endowment for International Peace, Washington, DC, 2000, especially chapters 6 and 7.

it provided the legal basis for a US military presence on Taiwan, eventually including nuclear weapons. Chinese perceptions that, despite US nuclear threats, the Soviet Union had been very timid about supporting China through invoking their 1949 mutual security agreement, is said to have been a significant factor in Mao's decision in mid 1955 that China had to acquire its own nuclear weapons. Three years later, in August–October 1958, hostilities between China and Taiwanese forces on Quemoy and Matsu erupted again. On this occasion, the crisis was shorter and less intense, although it did involve a letter from the Soviet leader, Nikita Khrushchev, informing his US counterpart, Dwight D. Eisenhower, that an attack against China would be regarded as an attack against the Soviet Union. It would appear that the Chinese regarded this as meaningless bluster when circumstances made it quite safe to make such threats, so Moscow got little credit for the gesture.

The Richard Nixon/Henry Kissinger initiative to re-connect with China in 1971–72 involved tortuous negotiations and, ultimately, some Delphic wording on Taiwan's position between the two states.[27] In the Shanghai Communiqué, issued during Nixon's visit, the crucial one-China principle was phrased as follows: 'The United States acknowledges that all Chinese on either side of the Taiwan Strait maintain that there is but one China and that Taiwan is a part of China. The United States Government does not challenge that position.'

Although the US initiative meant that China's seat at the United Nations now went to Beijing and that the establishment of full diplomatic relations between Washington and Beijing was foreshadowed, the language of the communiqué still left hanging just where the government of China actually resided. And while the communiqué also recorded US assurances that it would not encourage Taiwan's independence and would seek to constrain the quality of Japanese ties with Taiwan, it was again ambiguously worded on the issue of whether a peaceful resolution of the issue was a US preference or something closer to a US requirement. The issue here, of course, was whether the United States would contest any effort to re-integrate Taiwan by force.

This nebulous compromise was necessitated in part by Nixon's assessment of the domestic political opposition that he would encounter, but also by the more strategic thought that the United States should not be seen by the world as having been coerced by China (or anyone else) into 'abandoning' an ally. China has pressed the United States relentlessly to make its disengagement from Taiwan more absolute. In a further communiqué in 1982, the Reagan Administration agreed, in broad terms, to scale back US arms sales to Taiwan to the minimum necessary for defence.

---

27   An excellent source of detail on the vicissitudes of US-China relations over the period 1972–98 is Mann, *About Face: A History of America's Curious Relationship with China, from Nixon to Clinton.*

These undertakings have left ample scope both for Chinese complaints that the United States was going back on its word and for shifts in emphasis on the part of the Americans, whether as a reflection of changes in the balance of political power in Washington or to discourage aspirations in either Beijing or Taipei that the United States regarded as unhelpful or destabilising. In the 1990s, the United States characterised its approach as one of strategic ambiguity. The policy objective was to leave Beijing with the sense that the United States might come to the defence of Taiwan, and Taipei with the sense that it might not.

In the lead-up to Presidential elections late in 1995, pro-independence sentiments in Taiwan appeared to be on the rise, and the prospects for the pro-independence candidate, Lee Teng-hui, looked good. Beijing evidently concluded that the Taiwanese electorate needed a direct reminder of the price it would pay if it indulged these sentiments. The PLA conducted a series of major military exercises in the Taiwan Strait, including missile tests with a splash-down area just to the north of Taiwan. Coincidently, the Clinton Administration bowed to Congressional pressure and approved an informal visit by Lee to Cornell University, his alma mater. Beijing deemed this to be a violation of the ground rules regarding 'official' contact between Taiwan and the United States (and the US Department of State concurred) and probably saw it as tacit US endorsement of independence (which constituted a more serious violation of the undertakings given by the United States in the Shanghai Communiqué). The United States, in turn, saw the missile tests in particular as unduly provocative, and determined that it was timely to give the policy of strategic ambiguity a concrete reference point, that is, to go beyond even the explicit warnings it had conveyed through diplomatic channels. Two aircraft carrier battle groups (one returning from the Persian Gulf) were overtly redeployed to areas proximate to Taiwan to signal, successfully, US resolve regarding a peaceful resolution of the Taiwan question.

As a presidential candidate in 1992, Clinton had taken a hard line in respect of China in response to the suppression of protesters in Tiananmen Square on 4 June 1989. This negative attitude basically informed Washington's approach to Beijing throughout his first term and into the second. In June 1998, visiting China for the first time after over six years in office, Clinton used a joint press conference with Jiang Zemin, carried live on Chinese television, to charge that the use of force in Tiananmen Square had been 'wrong'. On the other hand, Clinton used the visit to reiterate publicly assurances on Taiwan that he had privately conveyed to Jiang Zemin during the crisis of 1995–96: the United States would not support Taiwan's independence, its admission to the United Nations or the creation of two Chinas.

The Bush Administration came to office in 2001 critical of the policy of strategic ambiguity and disposed to tilt toward making US support for Taiwan unambiguous. In April 2001, shortly after the two governments had worked through a collision in international airspace between a US intelligence-gathering aircraft and a Chinese fighter, Bush found an opportunity to declare informally, but publicly, that the United States would do 'whatever it takes' to assist Taiwan in defending itself.

In the Congressionally-mandated *Quadrennial Defense Review*, released two weeks after the 11 September 2001 terrorist attacks but, as a practical matter, still the only major policy document on national security crafted before these attacks, the Administration signalled an emphatic switch of US interest and concern toward Asia and China. After 11 September, with US priorities completely re-ordered and China proving to be helpful in practical ways in the global 'war on terror', the United States reverted to a more even-handed approach on Taiwan, insisting that both sides should protect the status quo and demonstrating a readiness to overtly oppose Taiwanese initiatives (particularly one calling for a referendum on seeking membership of the United Nations) as disturbing the status quo.

Although the Taiwan question has lost some of its immediate potency as a 'flashpoint', its intrinsic characteristics suggest that it remains an issue that merits the closest attention. First, both China and the United States see themselves as having compelling, if intangible, interests at stake in the manner in which the issue unfolds. China's Communist leaders have placed a great deal of weight on restoring the nation's honour and ensuring that others respect China's core interests. The restoration of full sovereignty over all territories claimed by China has been a core mission and a key indicator of the effectiveness and legitimacy of the regime. The end of the Cold War, if anything, heightened the importance of this nationalist mission, as the regime continued to lack democratic legitimacy while building socialism became a discredited and compromised raison d'être. For the United States, Taiwan is a similarly vital stitch in the fabric of its status as the world's pre-eminent state and, in Asia, as the chief architect and ultimate guarantor of the region's security arrangements. For nearly 60 years, the United States has 'required' that the issue be resolved without the use of force, and the ramifications of being seen to step away from this position would be far-reaching.

Second, there is a decisive military as well as political difference between deterring and, if necessary, defeating any Chinese attempt to take Taiwan by force, and reversing any successful Chinese occupation of the island. This simply means that any crisis will be characterised by powerful instincts on all sides to put their armed forces on a very short fuse. Third, geography tells us that it will be extremely difficult for a US-China conflict over Taiwan to be contained or limited. The Pentagon's response to the Taiwan crises of the 1950s illustrates that China's physical proximity generates military imperatives to widen any conflict. Finally, as China's economic capacities have flourished over the past 30 years, the modernisation of its armed forces has been moved up the list of national priorities, particularly since the mid 1990s. And the PLA's initial capability aspiration is to be able to prevent or to make sufficiently costly any US intervention on behalf of Taiwan that Washington will be deterred from doing so. The Pentagon has made clear that it is alert to the growing challenge to the US position in respect of Taiwan.

Taiwan is not in itself a sufficiently large strategic prize to push either party into war. The United States and China, however, are in an intensifying strategic competition, and Taiwan is most strongly symbolic of a distribution of power and influence that China remains resolved to change.

China's aspiration to have greater freedom in how it deals with Taiwan should not be equated with a preference to use force and to settle the matter sooner rather the later. We have noted on several occasions earlier in this paper that China attaches high importance to the quality and manner of its revival as a great power. It has consciously shed its image as a dissatisfied, rebel state in favour of painstakingly re-establishing itself as a comprehensively powerful state that is admired and respected—a state that can advance its interests through the weight of its economy, its soft power assets, and the potential of its armed forces. For such a China—a China that sees itself as recovering its rightful place among the world's great powers—even the extreme vigilance that Beijing deems necessary to deny Taiwan any form of visibility on the international scene is probably a source of discomfort to many in its policy circles. But the loss of face in having to use force to prevent Taiwan's independence would be immeasurable.

In short, there are grounds for confidence that the United States and China will share a strong interest in maintaining the status quo in respect of Taiwan. That said, Taiwan remains the issue most likely to channel the broader suspicions and uncertainties in Washington and Beijing about whether and how they can fit together over the longer term into a focused and militarised standoff that could well set the tone for their wider relationship.

Korea

For some 50 years after the 1950–53 Korean War, US resolve to preclude the forceful re-unification of the peninsula by North Korea (and, at one remove, the Soviet Union and China) was a key determinant of America's military posture in North Asia. North Korea remained on a war footing after the 1953 armistice, and sustained an unrelenting belligerence toward the South and its superpower ally. The Soviet Union and China supported this posture through judicious economic and military assistance, seeking to protect the viability of North Korea, but to deny it the option of deciding independently to resume the war against the

South. They also offered political support through refusing to recognise South Korea and insisting that there should be just one seat for Korea in the United Nations—a seat that should be filled by North Korea. Their joint support for North Korea in the 1950s transformed into a competition for influence after the Sino-Soviet split in 1960—a development that North Korea was able to exploit to its advantage.

The United States based substantial ground and air forces, including tactical nuclear weapons, in South Korea throughout this period and developed elaborate plans for the rapid reinforcement of these forces from Japan and the continental United States. North Korea has sustained a prodigious military effort. It has more than a million people in uniform and some 70 per cent are deployed in the 250 km deep band of the peninsula between Pyongyang and the demilitarised zone (DMZ) that constitutes the border. The DMZ is barely 30 km from Seoul and North Korea has exercised the option of deploying many thousands of artillery pieces and rocket systems within range of the South Korean capital. To strengthen deterrence, and to reassure its South Korea allies, the United States persevered with deployment arrangements for its forces that ensured that even focused and limited North Korean aggression would put US lives at risk and increase the certainty of triggering US involvement in resisting the aggression. The circumstances that created and sustained extreme belligerence across perhaps the most highly militarised border in the world began to be dislodged with the end of the Cold War. Even so, the military standoff on the Korean peninsula had become so entrenched and so calcified that it has proved surprisingly resistant to nearly two decades of post-Cold War developments.

The Soviet Union, under Mikhail Gorbachev, took the initiative in 1990–91 to open diplomatic relations with South Korea and to abandon its opposition to both Koreas being represented in the United Nations, symbolically erasing even the pretence of a legitimate North Korean claim to lead a re-unified Korea. China followed the Soviet lead in 1992. Unfortunately, this decisive disengagement by its two large socialist benefactors appears only to have stiffened North Korea's resolve to stay the course. It probably also strengthened North Korea's determination to acquire nuclear weapons and long-range ballistic missiles as it became apparent to Pyongyang that sustaining the effectiveness of its massive army with minimal external support was beyond its capacities. It seems likely that North Korea's absolute resistance to change, especially on the economic front (which would include greater receptivity to doing business with the South and supporting adjustments in its foreign and security policy settings) ultimately persuaded Russia and China that it was a liability they could live without. It was to be a consequential development.

In 1992, the United States withdrew all its remaining nuclear weapons from South Korea (reportedly 192 of them), pursuant to an agreement with Russia to bring all forward-deployed sub-strategic nuclear weapons back to their respective national territories. The two Koreas appeared to capitalise on this development by concluding a bilateral agreement in January 1992 to keep the peninsula free of nuclear weapons and the means to make them, with each side permitting the other to verify compliance with this undertaking. Later in the same year, Pyongyang's difficulties in living up to its Non-Proliferation Treaty (NPT) obligations—specifically, the degree of transparency requested by International Atomic Energy Agency (IAEA) inspectors—began. It initiated procedures to withdraw from the NPT and reached an eleventh hour deal with the United States in October 1994 to freeze its nuclear program in exchange for a regular supply of fuel oil and the construction of two 1000 megawatt light water power reactors. Under this 'Agreed Framework', the new reactors would be completed and come online only after more permanent arrangements had been agreed to dismantle those North Korean capacities that could contribute to a weapons program.

The Agreed Framework held together, if only barely, until October 2002 when the Bush Administration accused Pyongyang of violating the agreement by secretly developing a uranium enrichment capacity to give North Korea an alternative to the plutonium-based bomb program that it had agreed to freeze. Events escalated quite dramatically. North Korea expelled IAEA inspectors monitoring the freeze, the United States suspended fuel oil shipments (and, later, work on the two power reactors), North Korea withdrew from the NPT and, by mid-2003, the six most directly concerned states (the United States, China, Japan, Russia and the two Koreas) found themselves in the so-called Six-Party Talks seeking to reverse Pyongyang's all but declared intent to acquire nuclear weapons. This effort failed, with North Korea becoming the eighth state in the world to conduct a nuclear test in October 2006.

This is not the place to give an account of the Six-Party Talks process. Our interest lies primarily in what developments on the Korean Peninsula suggest and foreshadow about China's relations with the United States. During the 1990s and into the new century, the position of both North and South Korea between these two giants underwent almost revolutionary change. When China effectively ditched Pyongyang in favour of Seoul, the relationship with the latter flourished quite dramatically. Trade and investment flows grew strongly, while the political relationship not only matured but achieved a noticeable degree of comfort. Coincidentally, public attitudes in South Korea toward North Korea underwent a marked transformation, with negative memories of the war and of a continuing acute threat giving way to perceptions of kinship and a propensity to discount the threat. In addition, South Korea's strong economic performance since the 1970s had allowed Seoul to acquire a genuinely potent defence capability. These several developments contributed to a significant qualitative change in South Korean attitudes toward the United States and the South Korea-US alliance in the direction, naturally, of a weakened sense of dependence on the United States and less tolerance of both the irritations associated with the US military presence and of US pressures to sustain common or at least complementary policies, particularly toward North Korea.

As part of its broader initiative to 'transform' its conventional military forces, but also to respond to the new political climate between Washington and Seoul, the United States has reduced its forces stationed in South Korea, is redeploying its forces out of Seoul and away from the area between Seoul and the DMZ, and has pressed South Korea to assume some of the most taxing roles in the event of aggression from North Korea (particularly the prompt suppression of all those rocket and artillery systems within range of Seoul). In addition, the arrangements (in place since the 1950s) that would place South Korean forces under US command in the event of war will end in 2012. A further important element of this re-modelling of the US-South Korea alliance is that the United States is restructuring its remaining forces to make them lighter and easier to deploy and sustain in operations *beyond* the Korean Peninsula.

The changed dynamics in South Korea's relations with both the United States and China have been reflected in the Six-Party Talks. South Korea has often found China's priorities and preferred approaches to North Korea more in sympathy with its own interests than those of the United States. For Washington, the exclusive objective has been to erase Pyongyang's capacity to build nuclear weapons. China certainly shares this interest but attaches far more importance to precluding any sudden, destabilising change in North Korea that could be difficult to control and which could result in a continuing strong role for the United States and Japan in a reunified Korea. Protecting the regime in North Korea, sustaining its capacity to act as buffer between the United States and China and relying on China's proximity to bring a reforming North Korea (re-unifying gradually with the South) securely into China's sphere of influence looked much more attractive to Beijing.

These differing priorities bedevilled the Six-Party Talks, not least by offering scope to Pyongyang to manoeuvre between the other camps. Beijing was at pains to deny that it had significant leverage over Pyongyang and sought to sustain, for as long as possible, the contention that it was merely a facilitator for negotiations centred on the United States and North Korea. In the event, Pyongyang's preparedness to test the boundaries of Beijing's preference to see the regime remain in place led China to become increasingly overt in its demands for more reasonable behaviour on the part of North Korea. Finally, in respect of North Korean threats to conduct missile tests in July 2006 and then a nuclear test in October, Beijing elected not to be discreet about its strong high-level protests, only to be humiliated by Pyongyang's rejection of these warnings.

Many were surprised that Pyongyang would bite the hand of the closest thing it had to a friend. What has probably been overlooked or discounted is that North Korea may always have had profound reservations about undue reliance on China for its security. The United States and Japan may be the primary contemporary enemies (that is, in the twentieth century), but for the preceding millennia China had been Korea's mortal enemy. It can be surmised that being 'downgraded' by Beijing in 1992 refreshed these historical memories and that Pyongyang's eventually unshakeable determination to get nuclear weapons was intended not only to diminish the risk of coercion by the United States but reflected also a deep-seated preference to be 'buffered' from China.

The consequences for North Korea of humiliating China have included closer and more effective policy coordination between Washington (which controls most of the carrots) and Beijing (which controls the more obvious sticks). The academic debate in China (presumed to be officially sanctioned) reflects a new appreciation that protecting the regime in Pyongyang, helping to ensure minimal societal stability in North Korea and reversing the nuclear program may not be compatible objectives, and that China will have to choose.[28] Some Chinese academics are prepared to speculate, privately, that Beijing has already signalled Pyongyang to the effect that all options are now on the table, that is, that the survival of the Kim regime is no longer Beijing's first priority. It is most unlikely that Pyongyang was oblivious to this risk and much more likely that it concluded that it was a risk it had to take. It may even have been a step that it relished being in a position to take.

For our present purpose, the important conclusion to be drawn from this brief review of the Korean issue is that it is now a most unlikely 'flashpoint' in US-China relations. To the contrary, it is shaping up to be a point of cooperation, even of partnership, and may give rise to a standing forum to shape and manage the security affairs of Northeast Asia.

---

28 Bonnie Glasser, Scott Snyder and John S. Park, 'Chinese Debate North Korea', *PacNet Newsletter*, 8 February 2008, available at <pacnet@hawaiibiz.rr.com>, accessed 20 June 2008.

Chapter 3
China's Military Modernisation

The patient, methodical and pragmatic manner in which China has approached its economic and broad foreign policy objectives has, if anything, been even more conspicuous in the military sphere. The evidence supports the contention that shaping the evolution of the People's Liberation Army (PLA) was a vital component of Deng Xiaoping's grand strategy and that an 'understanding' between the political and military leadership held together amazingly well.

The uncertainty and speculation surrounding the sort of power that China could become, and on the extent of the adaptation of familiar arrangements and processes in the security arena that could become necessary to accommodate it, are encapsulated in the cautious but persistent debate that has arisen concerning China's military modernisation. This debate can roughly be traced back to the mid 1990s when China's announced military expenditures began to rise even faster than its Gross Domestic Product (GDP), suggesting a policy development of some significance.

Given China's long and turbulent history, including its recent past, it is no surprise to find that the military, presently the PLA, has always been a formidable political and bureaucratic force within the Chinese 'Establishment'. For the first three decades of the People's Republic of China (PRC), the government played to its one strength, manpower. Under Mao Zedong's doctrine of 'people's war', or guerilla war on a massive scale, the PLA envisaged conceding territory and lives in the process of gradually smothering an invader. The putative aggressor was the United States in the 1950s, the United States and the Soviet Union in the 1960s and then the Soviet Union alone in the 1970s and 1980s. Since the end of the Cold War, the United States has re-emerged ever more clearly, not so much as an overt enemy, but as the power that China aspires to match in terms of economic strength and political influence, and to neutralise in terms of coercive military capacity.

To give effect to Mao's Cold War strategy, PLA strength hovered at around 5 million. This was by far the largest standing army in the world, with correspondingly formidable numbers of major weapon systems, particularly tanks, artillery, combat aircraft and submarines. Moreover, the armed forces consumed an onerous share of GDP, around 15 per cent in the mid 1960s. Despite this lavish funding (which was due also to the PLA's central role in maintaining internal security and the exclusive primacy of the Chinese Communist Party (CCP)), the PLA never approached the status of a 'modern' military force. After the defeat of Japan in 1945, and of their domestic rivals the Kuomintang in 1949, China's economic and military revival was nurtured by the Soviet Union, itself neither wealthy nor disposed to seeing China emerge as a serious competitor in any dimension within the Socialist bloc. Moreover, this link was severed abruptly in 1959–60, long before China's indigenous capacities in science, technology and industrial skills were capable of flourishing independently (even setting aside the convulsions of the Great Leap Forward and the Cultural Revolution). The result was that the PLA continued to be equipped through the 1980s with second-echelon Soviet military hardware from the 1950s.

Then came Deng Xiaoping with his transforming determination to place economic revival ahead of all other national imperatives, including ideology. Deng succeeded in 1978 in committing the CCP to focus as exclusively as possible on economic development, and to abandon the command economy in favour of the market economy, including international trade and investment. This was an extraordinary political accomplishment. Deng certainly had compelling internal empirical evidence to support his case for 'revolutionary' change in China's economic settings, but he would also have used the fact that China was being out-classed to the point of humiliation by its former mortal enemy (Japan), by its errant province (Taiwan) and by other neighbouring states like Hong Kong and South Korea that had for millennia aspired to match China's economic, social, scientific and technological accomplishments. For the Chinese, the enduring shorthand for this remarkable reversal in its posture toward the world has been 'the reform and opening up'.

The evidence would support the view that a critical development supporting Deng's new policy settings was what might be termed a 'grand bargain' with the PLA. As noted earlier, Deng's case for revolutionary change included the strategic assessment that the international environment was both favourable for China's core interests and could be expected to remain reliably stable. If these judgements were considered sound, it made giving absolute priority to economic development look like a judicious gamble. It could be inferred that Deng pointed to the robust stalemate that the superpowers had fallen into, namely that (since normalising relations with the United States) China was well placed to enhance deterrence by manoeuvring between them if necessary, and that China's earlier concerns about superpower collusion against China could now be discounted.

It would appear that Deng persuaded the PLA to come on board with the argument that, absent a revolution in China's economic circumstances, the PLA would be competing for a slice of a comparatively static national cake. Alternatively, it could accept being ranked fourth and last in Deng's list the national priorities (behind agriculture, industry, and science and technology) and to receiving a declining share of GDP, and regard this relative abstinence as an investment in building a robust economy which would, over the longer term, deliver the resources and national competencies needed to develop an internationally competitive military force.

This hypothesis is informed guesswork, at best, but the graph depicted in Chart 1 would seem to back it up. Chart 1 draws on data compiled by the *US Arms Control and Disarmament Agency* over the years 1966 to 2005, and published in *World Military Expenditure and Arms Transfers*. ACDA did changes its methodology occasionally, but provided overlapping data so that trends can still be clearly discerned.

Chart 1: Military Expenditure as Percentage of GDP, 1966–2007

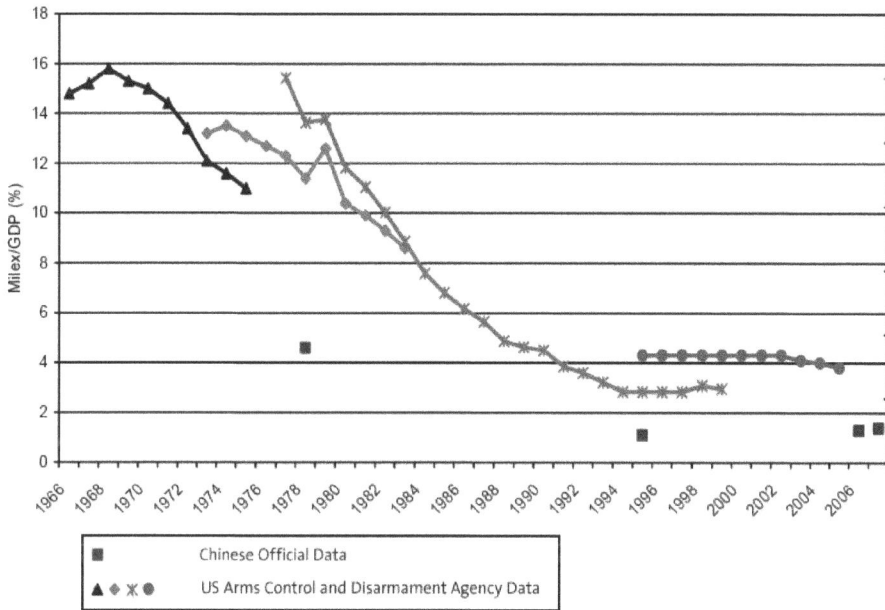

(*Sources: World Military Expenditure and Arms Transfers*, US Arms Control and Disarmament Agency (reports); *China's National Defense in 2008*, Information Office of the State Council of the People's Republic of China, Beijing, January 2009).

Trends of this scale and duration do not occur by accident: they are made to happen. It should be borne in mind however that, although ranking last, military modernisation was still in the top four national priorities. Moreover, the trends depicted in Chart 1 disguise an important reality. The success of the 'reform and opening up' proved to be so spectacular—an average annual rate of economic growth of nearly 10 per cent over the thirty years 1978–2008—that the military share of GDP could fall steadily while the absolute volume of resources devoted to the military actually continued to increase, at least in most years.

This is borne out by the official data set out in Table 2, and taken from the new Ministry of National Defense website. The respective trends in military expenditure and GDP resulted in the milex/GDP ratio falling from 4.6% in 1978 to 1.4% in 2007.

Table 2: Average Annual Growth Rates of Military Expenditure and GDP, 1978–2007 (current price)

	Mil. Expenditure	GDP
1978–87	3.5	14.1
1988–98	14.5	20.7
1998–2007	15.9	12.5

(*Source*: Ministry of National Defense (www.mod.gov.cn), accessed 13 November 2009)

The PLA leadership, aided by Deng's preparedness in 1985 to declare that a 'people's war' against an invading Soviet Union could no longer be regarded as a realistic scenario, was pushed to cut personnel numbers substantially in order to make the relatively constrained military budget 'go further'. One million personnel were cut between 1985 and 1987, another 500 000 between 1997 and 2000, and a further 200 000 between 2003 and 2005. Over the whole period, the PLA's personnel strength fell from 4.2 million to 2.3 million (although the paramilitary People's Armed Police roughly doubled in strength to 1.6 million over the same period, so the decline in the total number of 'military' personnel was more modest).

It would appear that the PLA's brief was both to accept a sharp diminution in its relative share of the nation's resources and to shift the focus of the resources it did have available away from strengthening immediate capabilities in favour of enhancing its capacities to develop, produce and make good use of modern weapon systems and equipment. In other words, with defence policy shifting progressively away from the land-based 'people's war' toward shorter, more limited engagements in high-technology maritime environments and the PLA endeavouring to institutionalise integrated air/land/sea operations, China's military–industrial–scientific complex set out to learn how to develop and produce advanced military equipment while minimising the costs of actually re-equipping the armed forces with successive generations of, at best, marginally better equipment. The evidence supports the contention that the PLA resisted the temptation to proliferate systems that it knew to be well below international standards and/or which were unduly dependent on critical components that China could not yet develop and produce indigenously and which had to be imported. In effect, during the 1980s and 1990s in particular, China focused on developing the submerged components of the military iceberg, while doing what it hoped would be just enough on the visible peak; that is, the PLA's order of battle.

China's Government has undertaken several reforms of the scientific-industrial sector supporting the PLA. Like governments the world over, it is seeking arrangements best suited to taking the PLA to the cutting edge and keeping it there: how to capture the benefits of competition; decide whether research and development (R&D) and production should be performed in the same or separate enterprises; how to allow the military sector to capitalise on technological developments in the civilian world without compromising security and secrecy, and so on. This has been an iterative process. Given that China started with mammoth state-owned defence industries still comfortable with decades-old Soviet military technology, and that the government as a whole remains deeply committed to control, protection and secrecy, external observers are severely handicapped in assessing how much progress has been made. The instincts that external observers develop on this issue, often driven by how much weight they feel can sensibly be placed on the occasional hard data point like the destruction of an orbiting satellite in January 2007, play a key role in shaping assessments of how soon China could become a serious military challenge to anyone and everyone in its immediate neighbourhood.

To return to Chart 1, it is clear that China's phenomenal economic growth since the late 1970s has softened the pain of the bargain the PLA struck with the political leadership. In addition, it would seem that the PLA spent the next two decades focusing relatively heavily on the scientific and industrial capacities needed to support a modern military force. By the mid-1990s, however, the political leadership began to loosen the purse strings. Military expenditure as a share of GDP stopped falling and even rose slightly in some years. This means that, for the past decade, China's military expenditure has increased by at least 10 per cent annually in real terms. By any standards, and particularly for a country that is not at war (even though it does consider that it is confronted with a major security crisis in that Taiwan could step beyond the very narrow boundaries that Beijing considers acceptable as not involving significant lose of face), this rate of growth in military expenditure signals a new urgency about enhancing China's military capabilities. For those who believe that China has made important progress on the scientific and industrial fronts, it means that major capability improvements should be anticipated sooner rather than later.[1]

---

1 For example, see Michael Pillsbury, 'PLA Capabilities in the 21st Century: How Does China Assess its Future Security Needs?', in Larry Wortzel (ed.), *The Chinese Armed Forces in the 21st Century*, Strategic Studies Institute, US Army War College, Carlisle, PA, December 1999, pp. 89–158, available at <http://www.au.af.mil/au/awc/awcgate/ssi/chin21cent.pdf>, accessed 16 November 2009.

The transparency question

Statistically, China seems a pretty normal state in terms of the resources it devotes to defence. In terms of military expenditure as a share of GDP or per head of population, armed forces as a proportion of population, and other possible indices, the Chinese figures all tend to fall well within the 'normal' range when compared to other states (especially, of course, if one makes commonsense adjustments or allowances for China's disproportionately large population).

The first dilemma, however, is that considerable scepticism surrounds the credibility of official figures. For the better part of two decades, from 1960 to the late 1980s, China published no information on military expenditure, not even a single number as its defence budget. Today, as was the case with the Soviet Union in the past, it is widely believed that official Chinese expenditure data exclude important categories of activity that are included in defence expenditure under Western accounting conventions.[2] The expenditures that various sources suggest are omitted range across paramilitary forces (especially the People's Armed Police), nuclear weapons, subsidies to defence industry, military R&D, defence imports, and military pensions.

In recent years, China has adopted the practice of issuing Defence 'White Papers'. These White Papers include long-winded and very general discussion about the roles and missions of the armed forces, but they are serious documents that the rest of the world has begun to study carefully. The White Papers also insist, quite explicitly, that just about every category of expenditure suspected by some foreign agency of being excluded from the official defence budget is in fact included in the official figures. The Chinese Government therefore directly contests the practice of supplementing its official figures with estimates of omitted categories of military expenditure to arrive at figures useful for international comparisons. Unfortunately, China has not relaxed the tight secrecy that surrounds its major resource allocation decisions. Although official Chinese documents insist that the National People's Congress is fully briefed on and approves total government expenditure, including defence expenditures, there are no visible internal processes requiring the leadership to expose and justify the full extent of the resources that flow to the military.[3] Nor has China

---

2   Many countries have entrenched institutional arrangements that make budget allocations to the 'Ministry of Defence' an incomplete picture of the state's defence or military expenditures. A simple example is that, in the United States, significant expenditure on nuclear weapons is to be found in the budget for the Department of Energy. In most cases, however, the governments concerned acknowledge and accept the validity of aggregating expenditures across a number of portfolios to arrive at a legitimate figure for the state's military expenditure.

3   For example, China's September 2005 White Paper, *China's Endeavors for Arms Control, Disarmament and Non-Proliferation* asserts on p. 14 that: 'Examined and approved by the National People's Congress, China's defence budget is open and transparent.' See 'Full text of White Paper on Arms Control', *China Daily*, available at <http://www.chinadaily.com.cn/english/doc/2005-09/01/content_474248.htm>, accessed 24 June 2009.

made its government expenditure or national accounts sufficiently detailed and transparent to allow outsiders to develop confidence in the integrity of the numbers through techniques like as input-output analysis. It should also be pointed out, of course, that the Chinese leadership cannot be transparent to the outside world in this respect or any other without also sharing information with its own people and this raises a whole range of additional considerations about the internal balance of power. So we have an impasse. China claims that it is being responsive to calls for more transparency, but there is little in the way of enlightenment.

In addition to estimating the real size of China's military expenditure in the local currency, analysts can employ different exchange rates to convert these numbers into a common currency. The major option is to use a purchasing power parity (PPP) rate rather than the official exchange rate on the grounds that China is still a developing economy and that the official rate reflects only the narrow band of the economy that is modernised and exposed to international competition. For the past twenty years or so, World Bank PPP estimates suggested that the Chinese currency was some four times stronger than the official exchange would suggest. This means that a given economic activity in China that is valued at A\$25 when converted at the official exchange rate becomes A\$100 of economic activity using the PPP rate. New World Bank estimates, compiled in collaboration with China and released in February 2008, conclude that the old figures overstated China's economy by about 40 per cent. In PPP terms, China remains the world's second largest economy, but is less than half the size of the US economy rather than the 70–80 per cent figure that had become commonplace in recent years. Similarly, projections that China would overtake the United States around 2020 will now have to be revised. All of this, of course, underscores the fact that the precision and credibility most people instinctively attribute to numerical information is often misplaced.

Finally, it is common practice to make international comparisons of economic data in constant prices; that is, adjusting for inflation in each country and comparing the aggregates in real terms. Once again, options are also available when making this adjustment for inflation, from the familiar Consumer Price Index (CPI) to the more arcane (unless you are an economist) implicit GDP deflator.

Taking all this together, one can find estimates of China's military expenditure that range from about double the official figure converted at the official exchange rate to over ten times this figure. To illustrate this point, we can compare figures

People's Republic of China, *China's Endeavors for Arms Control, Disarmament and Non-Proliferation*, White Paper, Beijing, September 2005, available at *China Daily*, available at <http://www.chinadaily.com.cn/english/doc/2005-09/01/content_474248.htm>, accessed 24 June 2009

75

from two established sources, the Stockholm International Peace Research Institute (SIPRI) and the International Institute for Strategic Studies (IISS). SIPRI supplements China's official figures for military expenditure with estimates for categories of expenditure not included, and converts total military expenditure and GDP to US dollars using the official exchange rate. The IISS also adds in estimated expenditure on military activities believed to be excluded from the official figures. It then estimates how much of the total is absorbed by personnel costs and operations and maintenance which it converts at PPP rates on the grounds that these expenses are largely divorced from the international sector of the Chinese economy. The remainder of the estimated total (composed mostly of procurement of weapons and equipment, and military R&D) is deemed to be more exposed to the international sector and is converted at the official rate. The IISS also employs estimates of China's GDP using PPP rates. The results are rather confusing. For 2005, SIPRI's estimate of total Chinese defence expenditure was US$41 billion which accounted for 2.4 per cent of GDP. For the same year, the IISS figure for military expenditure was more than twice as big at US$103.9 billion, but this larger figure accounts for a significantly smaller share of GDP (1.3 per cent).[4] The US Defense Intelligence Agency (DIA), however, estimates that China's military expenditure accounted for some 5 per cent of GDP in the early years of the new century—much higher than either the SIPRI or IISS estimates.[5]

Clearly, differences of this magnitude can colour broader assessments of the capability and rate of expansion of China's armed forces. Despite the fact that the military expenditure figures in circulation differ widely, and lose much of their apparent authority if one reads the footnotes on how they were constructed, these figures are very influential. Most observers feel more comfortable with this index of a country's military 'effort' than with assessments of the actual capabilities being acquired as a result of this effort. For one thing, assessments of capability are a very specialised business and, for another, these assessments tend to be even more varied in their conclusions than estimates of expenditure.

It is of some interest, therefore, that the RAND Corporation, one of the most respected security think-tanks in the United States, weighed in with a report in 2005 suggesting that some of the higher estimates of Chinese military spending constructed within the US Government were implausible. The RAND study suggested that omitted expenditures amounted to 40–70 per cent of the official budget (that is, the official figure should be multiplied by 1.4–1.7), and that, converted at PPP rates, China probably spent in the order of US$70 billion (or

---

4 See Stockholm International Peace Research Institute, *SIPRI Yearbook 2006*, Oxford University Press, Oxford, 2006, pp. 326–52 and International Institute for Strategic Studies, *The Military Balance 2008*, Routledge, London, February 2008, p. 445.

5 See the quoted remarks by Defense Intelligence Agency Director Vice-Admiral Wilson in Robert Wall, 'China Defense Budget Could Double by 2005', *Aviation Week & Space Technology*, 25 March 2002, p. 33.

2.3–2.8 per cent of GDP) annually on its armed forces in the early 2000s. In a possible dig at the DIA, the RAND study estimated that if military expenditure increased at the maximum feasible rate (which was not elaborated on), it could account for 5 per cent of GDP by the year 2025.

Perhaps for these reasons, the annual Pentagon report to Congress, *The Military Power of the People's Republic of China*, has, until recently, eschewed financial and economic data altogether. The Pentagon's report for 2007, however, states that the official Chinese figures exclude expenditure on the strategic forces, imported weapons and equipment, military R&D, and the paramilitary forces.[6] It also notes that China's official budget converted at the official exchange rate produces a military expenditure figure of US$45 billion for 2007, while the DIA estimate for the same year falls in the range of US$85–125 billion.[7]

In these circumstances, the most sensible approach for the analyst is to accept that absolute magnitudes cannot be reliably estimated and to be content with the trends that can be discerned in time series data computed on a consistent basis, like the data used to construct Chart 1. Chart 1 reflects the sustained implementation over more than 15 years of a political decision to put economic growth first and, as we have argued, of a grand bargain with the PLA to accept a sharp reduction in its share of a miserable economic pie in return for the promise of an appropriate share of a much larger and expanding pie at some point in the future. The bargain was reviewed in the mid 1990s to allow a significant acceleration in funding for the PLA.

Defence Doctrine and Force Posture

Mao Zedong's doctrine of 'people's war' played to China's limited strengths, had a strong resonance with socialist ideology and reflected deep-seated instincts of isolationism and rebellion against the prevailing international system. The scenario that dominated PLA thinking was a cataclysmic one: the invasion of China by a superpower, with the extensive use of nuclear weapons all but certain. Mao's dominance of China's political scene was such that, even after his death, political leaders had to be careful not to be seen to be trifling with his legacy. These circumstances highlight the enormity of Deng's political accomplishment in securing endorsement of his 'reforms and opening up' on the economic front just two years after Mao's death. On the defence front, Deng was a good deal

6   Office of the Secretary of Defense, *Annual Report to the Congress, Military Power of the People's Republic of China, 2007,* Washington, DC, 2007, available at <http://www.defenselink.mil/pubs/pdfs/070523-China-Military-Power-final.pdf>, accessed 24 June 2009, p. 25.
7   It should be stressed again that, to the extent these constructed estimates of China's military spending, and the share of GDP that they absorb, employ PPP conversion rates, we should expect significant revisions as the new World Bank figures flow into the calculations.

more cautious.[8] Even while Mao was alive, in mid 1975 Deng had remarked to a closed governmental audience that the PLA had become a massive, complacent and obsolete institution.[9] Publicly, however, after he assumed the leadership, he confined himself to a modest doctrinal adjustment—'people's war under modern conditions'—but one that opened the door to new and critical thinking about the roles and missions of the PLA. The PLA's poor performance—very nearly disastrously poor—in teaching Vietnam a 'lesson' in 1979 for invading Cambodia, whose government Beijing supported, would have energised this new thinking.

In the mid 1980s, Deng concluded, and felt secure enough to articulate, that the defining scenario—a major, probably nuclear, war with the Soviet Union— was no longer credible and encouraged the PLA to begin to look at dealing with limited (in respect of both geography and political objectives) but intense conflicts on China's periphery. This new imperative was brought into sharp and sobering perspective by Operation *Desert Storm* in 1991. The PLA was amongst the keenest students of this swift but absolute rout of the Iraqi armed forces by a US-dominated international coalition. With the end of the Cold War and the demise of the Soviet Union, the United States stood exposed as the defining world power, not least in military terms. Moreover, like the PLA, the Iraqi armed forces had a strong Soviet pedigree, adding to the salience of this conflict in terms of both the capabilities that the United States had displayed and the limitations of Iraqi doctrine and tactics. Within two years, in 1993, the PLA had formally adopted as its new aspiration *winning limited wars under high-tech conditions*.

The United States, of course, continued to move the goalposts on what modern conventional forces could accomplish, eventually committing itself, under the George W. Bush Administration, to a more systematic transformation of the US military to capitalise fully on the potential offered, in particular, by revolutionary developments in information technologies. By 2004–2005, following the campaigns in Afghanistan and the combat phase of Operation *Iraqi Freedom*, the PLA further refined its primary objective to winning local wars under conditions of informationisation. In addition, on this occasion, the PLA provided an indicative timetable, namely laying the foundations for a modernised military by 2010 and achieving 'informationised' forces capable of winning local wars by 2050. Some US assessments suggest that these indicative

---

8   Readers interested in a fuller discussion of Deng Xiaoping's strategic pronouncements and the new scope they offered to China's security community are referred to the opening chapters of Michael Pillsbury (ed.), *Chinese Views of Future Warfare*, National Defense University Press, Washington, DC, 1997, available at <http://www.au.af.mil/au/awc/awcgate/ndu/chinview/chinacont.html>, accessed 24 June 2009.
9   Deng Xiaoping, 'Speech to an Enlarged Meeting of the Military Commission of the Party Central Committee' (14 July 1975), *Selected Works of Deng Xiaoping*, Beijing, 1 July 1983, in Joint Publications Research Service, *China Report*, Foreign Broadcast Information Service, Reston, VA, 31 October 1983, p. 19.

dates are something of a smokescreen and that PLA strategies to be able to deter and, if necessary, prevent the United States from bringing its military assets into areas close to China involve a much shorter timeframe.[10]

As noted earlier, assessments of China's military capacities based on the number and quality of personnel, equipment levels, training, exercises, doctrine and so on, as well as on how quickly the PLA may be approaching its declared objective, vary markedly. Insofar as there is a mainstream view, it would probably be that the PLA is making impressive progress but still faces an enormous task in transitioning from a huge army focused on continental defence to a modern integrated force made up of substantial air and naval capabilities as well as ground forces, capable of joint operations focused on the maritime environment, with robust connectivity in command, control and communications, strong intelligence, surveillance and reconnaissance capabilities and so on.[11]

Earlier, we advanced the hypothesis that, consistent with the bargain struck with China's political leadership in the late 1970s, the PLA resisted the temptation to proliferate systems that it knew to be well below international standards and/ or which were unduly dependent on critical sub-systems that China still had to import. This was done to minimise undue strain on the Chinese economy as the 'reform and opening up' program got underway. It was also done, pursuant to Deng's exhortation that China had to hide its strengths and keep a low profile while it rebuilt its economy, to minimise the risk of generating concerns among the established major powers that might then pursue countervailing strategies that would distract China from its economic objectives.

It has been an essentially universal experience for numbers of combat systems to fall because the cost premium associated with successive generations of technologically-advanced weaponry has been too great to allow systems to be replaced on a one-for-one basis. In China's case, however, this trend has been particularly dramatic across most major weapon systems. In the case of combat aircraft, submarines and tanks, holdings have shrunk by 50 per cent or more over the past 15–20 years. Moreover, modern systems are still being produced in small batches so that, even with significant acquisition from abroad (particularly of combat aircraft), these declining trends are likely to continue. Blue-water

---

10   Roger Cliff, Mark Burles, Michael S. Chase, Derek Eaton, and Kevin L. Pollpeter, *Entering the Dragon's Lair: Chinese Antiaccess Strategies and Their Implications for the United States*, RAND Corporation, Santa Monica, 2007, available at <http://rand.org/pubs/monographs/MG524/>, accessed 24 June 2009.

11   See, for example, *Chinese Military Power, Report of an Independent Task Force*, Council on Foreign Relations, 2003, available at <http://www.cfr.org/content/publications/attachments/China_TF.pdf>, accessed 24 June 2009; and Colonel John Caldwell (USMC), *China's Conventional Military Capabilities, 1994-2004: An Assessment*, Center for Strategic and International Studies, Washington, DC, 1994.

surface warships have been an interesting exception to this pattern, with total holdings rising gradually from a low base of 22 in the early 1970s to over 70 by 2006.[12]

Chart 2: Tanks

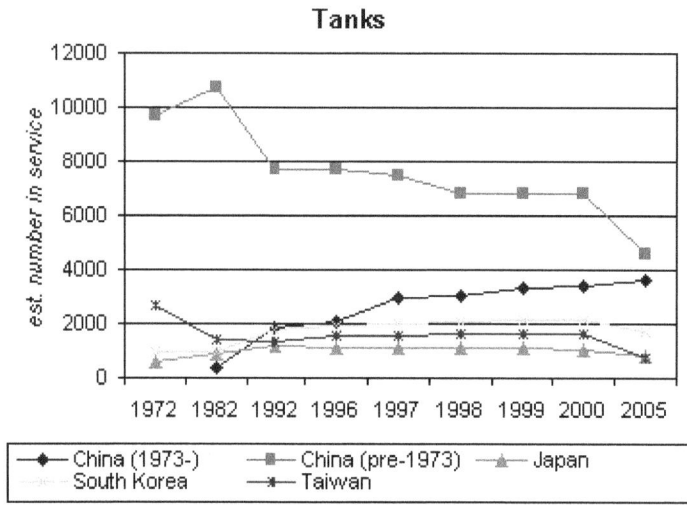

Chart 3: Combat Aircraft

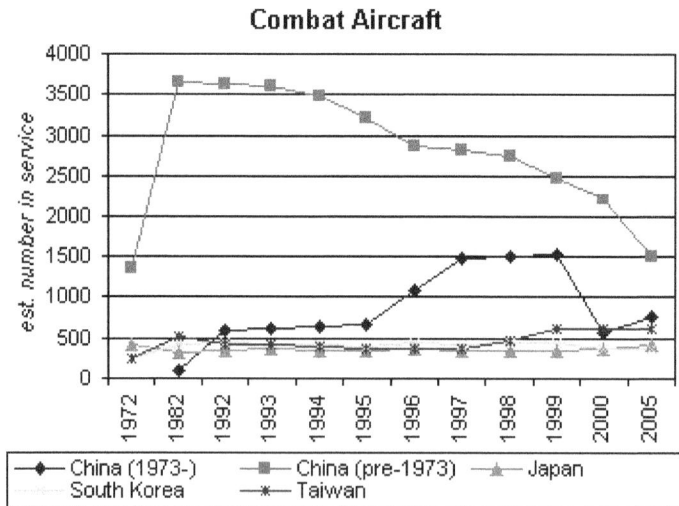

---

12   Frank W. Moore, *China's Military Capabilities,* Institute for Defense and Disarmament Studies, Cambridge, MA, June 2000, available at <http://www.comw.org/cmp/fulltext/iddschina.html>, accessed 24 June 2009.

Chart 4: Submarines (Tons)

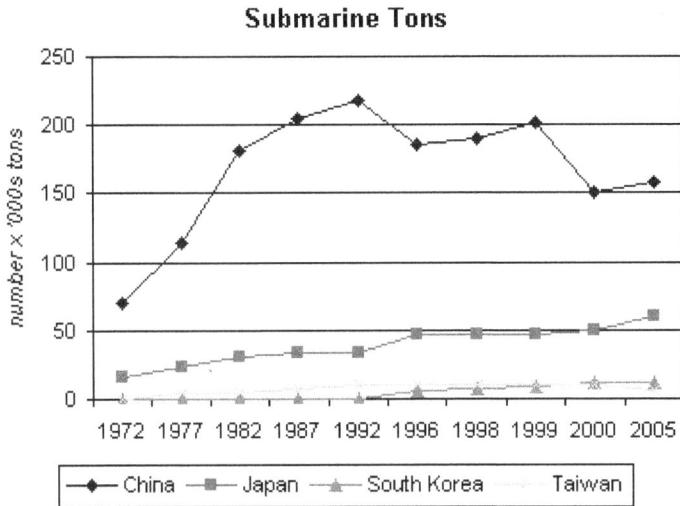

Submarine Tons

Chart 5: Surface Combat Ships

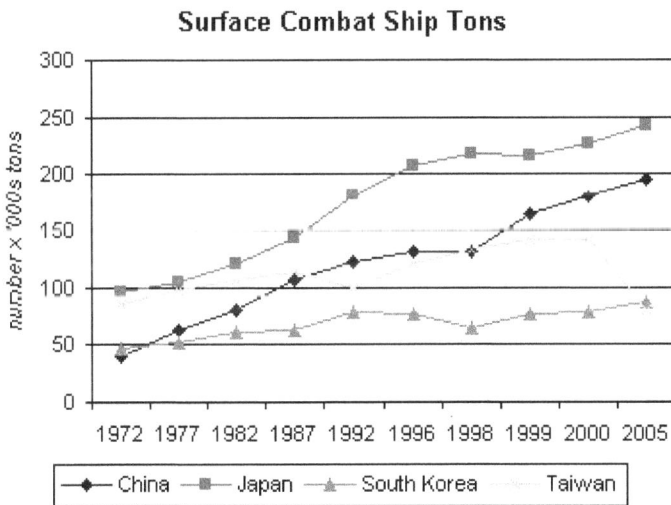

Surface Combat Ship Tons

(*Source for Charts 2–5*: Frank W. Moore, 'China's Military Capabilities', Institute for Defense & Disarmament Studies, Cambridge, MA, June 2000, available at <http://www.comw.org/cmp/fulltext/iddschina.html>, accessed 16 November 2009)

The 'fit' between the author's hypothesis and the evidence is not, of course, perfect. The political leadership appears to have resolved a long time ago that certain capabilities, although involving a long and costly development process, were so clearly indispensable to China's longer-term aspirations that they could not be deferred. Nuclear weapons are the most obvious example and are discussed more fully below. A strong capacity to exploit space, both for its military importance and its powerful symbolic association with great power status, is another.

A third exception is of a different kind and one that could be of defining importance. China's difficulties with Taiwan and, indirectly, the United States escalated steadily in the early 1990s until China's provocative missile tests in close proximity to Taiwanese territory and Washington's conspicuous deployment of two carrier battle groups in the waters southeast of Taiwan in March 1996 led to mutual disengagement. There is a widespread view that China's leadership determined at this point that it urgently needed more credible military capacities to back up its political rhetoric that it *would* use force to preclude any Taiwanese move toward independence. Some of the capabilities deemed appropriate for this purpose were within reach of China's defence industries, notably accurate, solid-fuel, short-range ballistic missiles. The number of these weapons deployed adjacent to Taiwan is now approaching 1000. Other imperatives, such as a credible capacity to establish air superiority over the Taiwan Strait or making the seas around Taiwan a hazardous environment for surface ships with anti-ship missiles launched from aircraft, submarines and surface ships were beyond China's capabilities, so Beijing had to resort to imports and production under licence. China turned to Russia for the systems it needed, including SU-27/30 combat aircraft, SA-10 long-range surface-to-air missiles, *Kilo*-class submarines and *Sovremenney*-class destroyers. This arms supply relationship was made politically imaginable by the end of the Cold War, and almost ordained by the coincidence of Russia's desperate economic circumstances and the arms embargo imposed on China by the United States and the European Union following the violent suppression of student protesters in June 1989.

The debate in Chinese military journals supports this Taiwan focus to military strategy. Non-Chinese observers have called this an anti-access strategy as the core objective is to deter, delay and, if necessary, defeat any US endeavour to come to Taiwan's aid.[13] An anti-access strategy is viewed as an asymmetric approach since the objective is not to out-muscle the forces the United States could bring to bear but to delay them, to deny them an opportunity to operate according to their preferences and, hopefully, to persuade them that 'rescuing' Taiwan would be disproportionately costly. The tactics being discussed include saturating the defences of aircraft carrier battle groups with missile attacks from land, sea and air platforms, including long-range land-based ballistic missiles with manoeuvring warheads that could put the carriers at risk well beyond the combat range of their aircraft. In addition, the Chinese are signalling their determination to focus on degrading the information connectivity between US

---

13   See Cliff, Burles, Chase, Eaton, and Pollpeter, *Entering the Dragon's Lair: Chinese Antiaccess Strategies and Their Implications for the United States.*

assets in space, on land, at sea and in the air. The anti-satellite capability China demonstrated in January 2007 was a particularly blunt signal to this effect. Finally, and disturbingly, some of the commentary in China's internal debate stresses that the imperative of keeping US forces as far away as possible places a premium on taking the initiative, that is, of striking first. Even though the capabilities being spoken of remain to a major extent aspirational, this internal debate illustrates both the potential for a crisis over Taiwan to escalate very quickly and the likely difficulty of confining hostilities to a particular geographic arena.

The reader will note the apparent contradiction between this decision in the mid 1990s to begin to accelerate the growth of China's military capacity and the simultaneous resolve discussed above to be more determined and creative in attenuating international concerns about an assertive and 'threatening' China. Governments, of course, often find themselves compelled to pursue contradictory policy objectives. In this case, it is reasonable to suppose that the directive, especially to the Foreign Ministry, to find ways of giving China a lower and more reassuring profile so as to prolong the window of opportunity to put economic growth first, simply presumed that everything possible would be done to minimise any damage to this posture that an 'inconsistent' acceleration on the military front might cause.

Nuclear forces

China detonated its first nuclear device in October 1964, becoming the fifth country in the world to do so. The Soviet Union initially provided decisive assistance. In particular, it transferred the gaseous diffusion technology for the enrichment of uranium—technology that the Soviet spies and sympathisers had secured from the US Manhattan Project. In the late 1950s, the Soviet Union had a change of heart and terminated its assistance, including reneging on a promise to provide China with the blueprints for a bomb. On the day of its first test, China also announced that it would never be the first to use these weapons and has retained this commitment ever since. China's nuclear forces, still innocuously located in the Second Artillery Corps, have developed very gradually over the ensuing 40 years. It has conducted just 45 tests (compared to around 1000 apiece for the United States and the Soviet Union) and most estimates place its total arsenal in the 200–400 range. At the same time, China has never been in the business of possessing token nuclear forces. China's arsenal is as diversified as its technological capacities have allowed and it remains determined to continue this process, especially in the direction of a reliable sea-based strategic nuclear deterrent (although the formidable anti-submarine capability that the United States developed during the Cold War is likely to see China's continuing primary reliance on land-based missiles).

China's geography requires re-thinking some of the terminology that has become entrenched since the days of the Cold War. The United States and the Soviet Union each acknowledged the other as the sole strategic opponent. Their geographic relationship led to nuclear delivery systems with a range in excess of 5500 km being classified as 'strategic', with shorter range systems variously labelled as 'sub-strategic', 'theatre' or 'tactical'. China has a more complicated geography and correspondingly complicated political histories with various neighbours. Thus, Chinese nuclear systems capable of reaching important targets in Japan, Russia, and India have to be considered at least a potential strategic nuclear deterrent against these countries. Indeed, in all three cases, a persuasive case could be made that China intends this to be the case.

China deploys about 20 liquid-fuelled full-range, single-warhead intercontinental ballistic missiles (ICBMs) (DF-5), capable of targeting all of the United States. The DF-5 was first deployed in 1981 and probably initially targeted against the Soviet Union. Just two were deployed in the 1980s, with the balance following in the 1990s. As a late-comer to the business of strategic nuclear deterrence, it would be reasonable to infer that China recognised from developments in the United States and the Soviet Union that the DF-5 did not represent a technology worth investing heavily in unless it was absolutely necessary. For one thing, liquid-fuelled missiles are cumbersome and dangerous to handle as well as vulnerable since it takes so long to prepare them for launch. Further, improvements in accuracy had led both superpowers to conclude that mobility offered greater assurance of survival than heavily protected but fixed launch silos. Clearly, broader assessments of China's strategic circumstances and the diminishing risk of war with a major power (not least the de facto alliance with the United States) allowed Beijing to conclude that it could get by with a modest number of DF-5s as an interim capability.

By 2007, a prolonged development process had yielded a solid fuel, mobile ICBM (DF-31) that was nearing operational deployment. It appears that China had some difficulty achieving the range capability that it desired and that a second variant, the DF-31A (or the DF-41 in some sources), has been developed to overcome this limitation. US ballistic missile defence deployments are expected to put upward pressure on whatever force levels China is planning for in the coming years, and is likely to intensify consideration of placing multiple warheads on its longer-range systems, something considered to be within China's current capabilities.

China has also patiently pursued a sea-based strategic deterrent capability despite encountering persistent development problems. It has for many years deployed a single submarine equipped to carry 12 JL-1 missiles (derived from the DF-21A with a range of about 1800 km), but its operational status has always been a matter of conjecture. Indeed, US intelligence asserts that it has never conducted an operational patrol. China is believed to be constructing perhaps three new missile submarines (SSBNs), the *Jin* Class, and has derived a new submarine-launched ballistic missile (SLBM) from the DF-31 program. This new missile, the JL-2, has a significantly longer range than its predecessor—possibly 8000 km against 1800 km—which will vastly increase the ocean spaces in which the launch platform can hide while still remaining within range of its targets. A great deal of uncertainty seems to surround the maturity and imminence of this new capability. Both the new SSBN and the JL-2 missile have been spoken of for a number of years, suggesting that China continues to experience serious difficulty in bringing these systems to operational status.

China possesses somewhat more numerous (over 70) intermediate and medium-range nuclear-capable missile forces able to put at risk targets in India, Japan, most of Russia, and Guam (a US possession in the Western Pacific that is undergoing a major revival as a forward military base). Roughly half of these missiles are older, liquid-fuel systems (DF-3A and DF-4), but the remainder consist of DF-21As, China's first solid-fuel, land-mobile medium range (2150 km) ballistic missile. All of China's long-range missiles carry a single high-yield warhead (around 3 megatons), except the DF-21A which is probably much more accurate and is believed to carry a 200–300 kiloton warhead. China also has a modest number (roughly 100) of aged medium bombers dedicated to the role of delivering nuclear weapons. As aircraft are the most versatile (and also the most vulnerable) nuclear delivery system, many analysts believe that the primary role of these bombers is the delivery of tactical nuclear weapons that, generally speaking, have smaller yields than those with a 'strategic' purpose. Still, these nuclear-capable aircraft are deployed at air bases within range of Japan, South Korea and Taiwan and can be armed with bombs of all yields.

China is particularly tight-lipped about its thinking on the roles and missions of its nuclear weapons. Its official documents stress its 'no first-use' pledge and the purpose of deterring both the use of nuclear weapons and the employment of coercive threats to use the these weapons against China. Like other nuclear weapon states, however, China has an interest in maximising the utility of nuclear weapons in protecting and advancing its interests. This cannot be done in complete secrecy. Potential adversaries have to be given signals about capabilities and the possible roles and missions that China envisages for its nuclear weapons. China squares this circle by authorising writings and debate about these issues that knowledgeable outsiders can assess as too likely to represent official thinking to be ignored, but which, of course, remain deniable.[14]

Chinese doctrinal literature suggests that China's nuclear forces have three core missions: (1) deterrence of the use or threat of use of nuclear weapons against China; (2) supporting China's conventional forces; and (3) delivering a nuclear counter-attack.

This literature also points to a priority list of effects that China's nuclear forces should seek to achieve if a conflict crosses the nuclear threshold, that is, if the adversary initiates the use of nuclear weapons. The effects are as follows:

- cause the will of the enemy (and its populace) to waver;
- destroy the enemy's command and control system;
- delay the enemy's war (or combat) operations;
- reduce the enemy's force generation and war-making potential; and
- degrade the enemy's ability to win a nuclear war.

With respect to US-China relations, China's 20 DF-5A missiles are generally considered to constitute a posture of *minimum deterrence*. Given that some of these might be lost in the enemy's initial strike with nuclear weapons, that a certain percentage are likely to malfunction, and that, looking to the future, some warheads might be intercepted by ballistic missile defences, this constitutes a modest number. These weapons carry an awesomely large warhead (3–4 megatons or over 200 times more powerful than the bombs dropped on Hiroshima and Nagasaki), and they are relatively inaccurate (which means that they can sensibly be targeted only at large cities). Whatever concerns China's leaders may have about how secure or reliable their ability to retaliate against the US mainland really is, deterrence still functions because their US counterparts can be presumed in most imaginable circumstances to require *certainty* that not a single Chinese warhead would get through.

The priority list for nuclear counter-attacks points to a more complex nuclear doctrine than the crude simplicity of a posture of minimum deterrence in respect of the United States. These objectives (especially those noted in the second, third and fourth bullet points above) clearly refer to China's nuclear capabilities that are sub-strategic in the US-China context, but which send a graphic message

---

14 The details on nuclear doctrine that follow are taken from Larry M. Wortzel, *China's Nuclear Forces: Operations, Training, Doctrine, Command, Control, and Campaign Planning*, Strategic Studies Institute, US Army War College, Carlisle, PA, May 2007, available at <http://www.strategicstudiesinstitute.army.mil/pdffiles/PUB776.pdf>, accessed 16 April 2008.

to the states in China's neighbourhood that might conceivably be involved in threatening its core interests, whether independently or in association with the United States.

Looking at the nuclear arena from the US perspective, the broad cycles in US-China relations are echoed in how China figured in US planning for the use of nuclear weapons.[15] During the 1950s, even though the US nuclear arsenal was expanding and diversifying at a dizzying pace, the United States was still coming to terms with this new capability. Plans for its use focused on supporting the public posture of massive retaliation against the Soviet Union in the event that it moved against Western Europe. The United States did have nuclear capabilities in the Pacific and, in the context of the Korean War and the two serious crises in the Taiwan Strait in 1954–55 and 1958, it chose to signal the availability of this option in its endeavours to shape the course of the crises in favourable directions.

In 1960, the United States consolidated its primary nuclear use plans into a Single Integrated Operational Plan (SIOP). The first iteration of this plan (which has been continually amended and remains an active document) included some targets in China as part of massive retaliation against the Soviet bloc. Two years later, China was separated from the Soviet Union and subject to more complex planning, although the presumption remained that any hostilities would involve both the Soviet Union and China as opponents. By the mid 1960s, the United States accepted the permanence of the Sino-Soviet split and, in 1967, the SIOP options had been refined to allow nuclear attacks against China that posed no threat to the Soviet Union. In 1982, a decade after re-engagement with the United States, China was dropped from the SIOP as a primary strategic nuclear target (although it remained subject to a separate and smaller nuclear war plan) on the grounds that the Soviet Union was so clearly the common enemy. Washington accepted that it made no sense for the United States to both plan to assist China in the event of Soviet aggression (which the Pentagon was directed to do) and to organise its nuclear forces to be able at all times to execute major strike options against China. Fifteen years later, in 1997, and just as the second Clinton Administration was leaning more strongly toward positive engagement of China, China was quietly re-instated in the SIOP as a primary strategic nuclear target. Clearly, one has to look beyond China's nuclear posture (which developed only marginally over this period) to explain this development, and to consider the deeper transformation in US and Chinese attitudes toward one

---

15   The material on this question is taken primarily from Hans M. Kristensen, Robert S. Norris and Matthew G. McKinzie, *Chinese Nuclear Forces and US Nuclear War Planning*, The Federation of American Scientists, and The Natural Resources Defense Council, November 2006, available at <http://www.nukestrat.com/china/chinareport.htm>, accessed 24 June 2009.

another after the demise of the Soviet Union and the growing certainty over the course of the 1990s that their relationship was destined to become the defining nexus in the twenty-first century.[16]

Assessment

Most analysts agree that it remains almost a nonsense to assess the military balance between the United States and China; their respective 'ballparks' do not as yet intersect. Naturally enough, however, China's military capacities look more formidable when set against its immediate ambitions for a credible capacity to use, or threaten to use, force in its neighborhood, above all, of course, to deter and if necessary contest any Taiwanese move toward independence.

Stepping back from the details of relative levels of military expenditure and from the balance of military forces, China still presents as something of an enigma. It is still, in some respects, a poor and weak developing country, and its diplomats are fond of deflecting calls for more genuine transparency by saying that transparency is an indulgence that only the rich and powerful can afford. At the same time, China deploys a modestly-sized but comprehensive nuclear force with a full range of warheads and delivery systems; it has a very serious and broad space program, including manned missions, that has major spinoffs for its military capacities; it has elected to develop and demonstrate a hit-to-kill anti-satellite capability which can also be seen as a precursor to ballistic missile defence systems; and its conventional forces can already lay claim to being the largest and most diversified in East Asia.

While responsible analysts may insist that it remains silly to compare the military capabilities of the United States and China, there can be little doubt that China takes it as given (and wants this to be recognised) that the United States is its natural benchmark in this arena as in others. China will be patient and methodical. It will not, through aggressively accelerating its military programs, risk either putting its economic development off balance or introducing counter-productive dissonance into its regional and global diplomacy. But it

---

16 One specific nuclear weapon development may have contributed to China being put back into the Single Integrated Operational Plan. Assessments of US intelligence material on a Chinese weapon test conducted in September 1992 led eventually to strong suspicions that China had somehow acquired design details on one of America's most sophisticated warheads—the W-88, eight of which can be deployed on a single *Trident* II SLBM, each with a yield of 445 kilotons, making it the most powerful warhead in the US arsenal. These suspicions led eventually to the Cox enquiry on the security of US weapon designs and focused on a Chinese-American scientist at the Los Alamos Laboratories. China's acquisition and mastery of this technology—a major advance even in the US context—would have strengthened US assessments that China intended eventually to leave minimum deterrence behind in favour of a more versatile nuclear posture. See Jeffrey T. Richelson, *Spying on the Bomb: American Nuclear Intelligence from Nazi Germany to Iran and North Korea*, W.W. Norton & Company, New York, 2006, pp. 414–18.

will aspire, painstakingly, to compare favourably with the United States in terms of the diversity of its military capacities and, by virtue of this, possess comprehensive denial capabilities vis-à-vis US armed forces in areas adjacent to China. China will, and indeed is, looking to asymmetric means to cope with US military strengths but, as a matter of honour and with an eye to the longer-term future, it is determined to play on the same chessboard as the United States. As one analyst put it, China is poised to demonstrate what a high-end asymmetric force posture might look like.[17] Desperate and demeaning shortcuts have no place in China's thinking: hence, perhaps, the demonstration of a 'hit-to-kill' anti-satellite capability and talk of using manoeuvrable ballistic missile warheads (with conventional, electro-magnetic or possibly nuclear payloads) to target aircraft carrier battle groups rather than, for example, extravagant language about waging total war by unconventional means to prevent Taiwan's independence.

Policy elites in Washington, both Republican and Democrat, have certainly recognised for some time that China's rise would become a transformational phenomenon. During the 1990s, the Clinton Administration preferred to acknowledge that China would become an influential strategic force, while characterising what it would take for this to be a positive development. US President Bill Clinton's *National Security Strategy* for 1999 spoke of China in the following terms:[18]

> A stable, open, prosperous People's Republic of China that respects international norms and assumes its responsibilities for building a more peaceful world is clearly and profoundly in our interests. The prospects for peace and prosperity in Asia depend heavily on China's role as a responsible member of the international community.

The Clinton Administration's equivalent defence statement, the 1997 Quadrennial Defense Review (QDR), while focused on the familiar regional threats in the Middle East (Iraq and Iran) and North Asia (North Korea), did acknowledge that US capabilities had been gamed against a possible regional great power or global peer that could emerge after 2015. Separately, it notes that 'Russia and China are seen by some as having the potential to be such competitors, though their respective futures are quite uncertain'.[19]

---

17   Robert D. Kaplan, 'How We Would Fight China', *The Atlantic Monthly*, June 2005, available at <http://www.theatlantic.com/doc/200506/kaplan>, accessed 24 June 2009.

18   President William J. Clinton, *A National Security Strategy for a New Century*, White House, Washington, DC, 1999, p. 36, available at <http://www.au.af.mil/au/awc/awcgate/nss/nssr-1098.pdf>, accessed 24 June 2009.

19   William S. Cohen, Secretary of Defense, *Report of the Quadrennial Defense Review*, Washington, DC, May 1997, p. 3.

The 2001 QDR, the only major statement on security policy prepared by the Bush Administration before the 11 September 2001 terrorist strikes on the United States, focused more specifically on China, although without linking it directly to the language used. The report notes:[20]

> Although the United States will not face a peer competitor in the near future, the potential exists for regional powers to develop sufficient capabilities to threaten stability in regions critical to US interests. In particular, Asia is gradually emerging as a region susceptible to large-scale military competition. The possibility exists that a military competitor with a formidable resource base will emerge in the region.

The next QDR, also prepared by the Bush Administration and released early in 2006, was more pointed and immediate, and less coy about China, noting:[21]

> Of the major and emerging powers, China has the greatest potential to compete militarily with the United States and field disruptive military technologies that could over time offset traditional US military advantages absent US counter strategies. Chinese military modernisation has accelerated since the mid-to-late 1990s in response to leadership demands to develop military options against Taiwan scenarios. The pace and scope of China's military build-up already puts regional military balances at risk. China is likely to continue making large investments in high-end, asymmetric military capabilities, emphasizing electronic and cyber-warfare; counter-space operations; ballistic and cruise missiles; advanced integrated air defence systems; next generation torpedoes; advanced submarines; strategic nuclear strike from modern, sophisticated land and sea-based systems; and theater unmanned aerial vehicles for employment by the Chinese military and for global export. These capabilities, the vast distances of the Asian theater, China's continental depth, and the challenge of en route and in-theater US basing place a premium on forces capable of sustained operations at great distances into denied areas.[22]

In just five years, in the Pentagon's view, the PLA developed from a 'possibility' that 'could emerge' into a force that was already putting 'regional military balances at risk'. And, although the PLA's ability to compete with the United

---

20 Donald H. Rumsfeld, Secretary of Defense, *Quadrennial Defense Review Report*, Washington, DC, 30 September 2001, p. 4.

21 Donald H. Rumsfeld, Secretary of Defense, *Quadrennial Defense Review Report*, Washington, DC, 6 February 2006, pp. 29-30, available at <http://www.defenselink.mil/qdr/report/Report20060203.pdf>, accessed 24 June 2009.

22 For a focused analysis of the issues alluded to in this quotation, see Cliff, Burles, Chase, Eaton and Pollpeter, *Entering the Dragon's Lair: Chinese Antiaccess Strategies and Their Implications for the United States*.

States remained a 'potential' development, when coupled with East Asia's geography and China's huge advantage in proximity, it is portrayed as presenting a quite pressing challenge to existing US military options.

It must also be pointed out that, prior to the 2006 QDR, the Bush Administration reverted to something resembling the Clinton formula. In September 2005, US Deputy Secretary of State, Robert B. Zoellick, gave a speech, identified as having been cleared with the White House, in which he invited China to consider becoming a 'responsible stakeholder' in the international system (and a co-author of future adaptations of this system), but also spelt out some of the more important ways in which China would have to change in order to qualify for this role.[23] The United States clearly saw this offer as a major gesture in the direction of acknowledging China's existing and prospective power and importance. The terms of the Zoellick speech have been discussed in senior US-China dialogue forums, and China's academics have enquired into the possible meaning of the terms 'international system' and 'responsible stakeholder'. China's leaders, however, have elected not to provide a substantive response to this proposal, a tactic consistent with the earlier observation that China is not yet ready to lock itself into commitments about how it proposes to fit into the international system.

---

23   Robert B. Zoellick, US Deputy Secretary of State, 'Whither China: From Membership to Responsibility?', National Committee on US-China Relations, 21 September 2005.

Conclusion

What are we to make of this short and eclectic enquiry into China's current resurgence? We are, in my view, past the point at which it makes sense to focus on assessing whether China will succeed in 'standing up' and resuming its place among the world's most consequential states. China's development into a mature contemporary state has a long way to run, but it has arguably completed its (re)-emergence, and it has the balance and robustness to sustain a strong, positive trajectory into the indefinite future. If everyone in East Asia is already very much aware of a compelling new force on the regional scene, one can only try to imagine how it will feel in the decades to come.

The striking feature of China's story over the past three decades is the degree to which the process has been engineered. Despite its immense size, China's transformation has been patiently, methodically and very deliberately constructed by a leadership group that has equally carefully protected its monopoly on power. Deng Xiaoping stands like a colossus over this process as the author of the enduring vision on where China should go and of the core guidelines that it should adhere to in order to get there. China's spectacular success is due overwhelmingly to Deng's far-sighted determination to immerse the country in the international system largely designed by and still presided over by the United States, a system that Mao Zedong's China had resolved to resist and, if possible, unravel. A question that has lurked in the back of some minds is whether China will continue to see strong advantage in helping to preserve and develop this system or begin to see itself as having outgrown the system and to lean toward more China-centric arrangements. East Asia's strategic trajectory will depend strongly on whether this distils into a bilateral contest to shape the regional order or whether both principals can be persuaded to prefer a more diffuse and collective shaping mechanism that also includes the likes of Japan and India.

China has worked hard and skilfully, and enjoyed considerable success, in recent decades to portray itself as a benign force, utterly absorbed in the task of lifting its mammoth population out of extreme poverty, and, as an integrated and increasingly interdependent member of the international community, doing so in a manner that produces major economic spinoffs for many if not most other members of the system. Chinese leaders have stressed that China needs and seeks maximum tranquility in its external relationships to avoid being distracted from this huge and long-term endeavour.

To this end, China has become one of the world's leading trading nations from within the World Trade Organization (WTO); it has stepped from well outside the Weapons of Mass Destruction (WMD)/long-range missile non-proliferation regime to membership of, and compliance with, the key instruments of this regime; it has become an enthusiastic proponent of addressing security challenges in multilateral forums like the ASEAN Regional Forum (ARF) and the Shanghai Cooperation Organisation (SCO); it has for a decade relentlessly promoted the principles of common and comprehensive security as its national security policy; the People's Liberation Army (PLA) has become the largest single contributor to UN peacekeeping operations; it has begun, cautiously, to recognise (in respect of Zimbabwe, Sudan and Myanmar) that its national interests are not served by resisting absolutely the emerging norm that the sovereignty of states is qualified by a 'responsibility to protect' the welfare of its citizens, and that the international community has rights and responsibilities in upholding this norm.

China's actions over the past three decades have accomplished a crucial qualitative change: broad impressions of China as a mysterious, somewhat exotic but also vaguely alien place have substantially given way to assessments in which 'normalcy' and 'similarity' dominate over 'difference'. In addition, we have noted above that China's leadership seems to attach a high priority to building the country's rise on broad and deep foundations, to ensure real substance and to minimise any vulnerabilities. To the extent practicable, short-cuts are avoided or at least abandoned if the longer-term penalties are recognised and assessed as damaging either to China's image or to the certainty of China's trajectory toward a nation of power and influence. It is reasonable to suppose, and to some extent inevitable in the Chinese context, that the leadership aspiration is to make this fourth resurgence in China's fortunes as substantive and durable as those in the past.

Finally, there is the fact that China's re-emergence is part of the evolution of an unfamiliar geopolitical environment—an environment in which several geographically dispersed and culturally distinctive countries will stand apart from the majority as disproportionately powerful but still subject themselves to the significant countervailing capacities of their peers. The more certain members of this 'group of giants' will be the United States, the European Union, China, Japan, Russia and India.

Taking these considerations together suggests that there is much to be said for the proposition that it is both valid and wise to take this 'new look' China at face value and to be confident that an ever more powerful and influential China will remain an agent of reassurance and stability and indeed become a 'responsible stakeholder' within the evolving international system.

There are, however, considerations that incline this observer toward a more cautious and circumspect assessment. First, there is China's size. Even for the most imaginative people, it is difficult to envisage the sort of entity that China will be in 25 or 50 years if it sustains anything like its present trajectory. While many see formidable challenges ahead for China on such fronts as the environment, pollution, and socially stressful income inequalities, few believe that its economic trajectory is unsustainable because of deep flaws in its economic fundamentals. In other words, China will, by any measure, become the largest economy in Asia quite soon, and eventually the largest in the world. Furthermore, China's economic strength will become progressively stronger and deeper in terms of attributes like its education system, its capacity to develop new technologies, and the magnitude and mobility of its capital resources.

Even if considerable doubt surrounds China's future standing in global terms at these future dates, there can be little doubt that China will be a dominant presence in East Asia and that the manner in which the United States, Japan and China fit together will be very different from the arrangements in place today. East Asia, of course, is the region of the world of greatest interest to Australia in economic, political and security terms. It follows that the manner in which the accommodation of China is approached and accomplished—whether the process leans toward the deliberate, collegiate and stabilising or is characterised more by suspicion, resistance and military competition—is a matter of fundamental concern to Australia.

These observations feed into a further set of considerations. Despite the enormity of China's economic and social transformation over the past three decades, its system of governance has proven to be highly resistant to change. China remains an authoritarian one-party state. Internal checks and balances on the authority of the government remain weak and uncertain. This, in turn, has consequences that will make it harder for the Chinese leadership to steer its preferred course. The comparative absence of internal checks and balances on the authority of the government will intensify instincts elsewhere to at least hedge against the emergence of a powerful China, whether through seeking to build the foundations for countervailing coalitions or accelerating the development of selected military capabilities (or both). Needless to say, while both responses are predictable and even sensible, they tend to make the prospects for a deliberate, collegiate and stabilising strategic transformation rather remote.

In a similar vein, the reassurance provided by China's current foreign and security policy settings is qualified by the fact that they are so clearly careful choices made by the leadership and the policy elite. The fact that China is an authoritarian one-party state leads inescapably to the sensation that the policy choices are a means to an end, and to perceptions of being manipulated to the benefit of China's longer-term aspirations. Apart from the glimpses (despite China's tightly controlled political and bureaucratic environment) that emerge on the scale of these aspirations, there is a strong propensity among some in other policy elites to 'fill in the blanks' and to press for more robust hedging, if not outright competition to deny China's presumed aspirations. For those that are sceptical, the question becomes how far has China entered into external arrangements or allowed internal changes that are genuinely 'costly' in the sense of limiting the state's freedom to pursue its aspirations?

The US experience provides a benchmark against which to illuminate these observations. For pretty much all of the twentieth century, the United States loomed ever more decisively as the pre-eminent power in every dimension of that elusive concept. Yet there is widespread agreement that the United States, uniquely, somehow combined disproportionate power with reassurance. Most of the world never feared that the United States would use its power to conquer or to subjugate, a quality that added immeasurably to America's status and influence. The United States managed to pull off this feat not because it consistently exhibited statesmanship and policy skills of the highest order, but because not using its power in this 'traditional' way was a vague national preference that US democratic processes could essentially impose on the leadership. It was not something that was left up to the policy elites to decide. Somehow, it would appear, this intangible quality was transmitted to and imbedded itself around the world.[1]

It can be accepted that the introduction of such factors as market economics, the advent of economic opportunity, labour mobility, international travel and widespread exploitation of the Internet have transformed China's internal atmosphere dramatically in the last 30 years. It is a much freer society than it used to be. Many analysts go on to express confidence that the Chinese Communist Party has unleashed forces that will prove impossible to guide, let alone slow or stop, and that political pluralism is inescapable. I would submit, however, that China's accumulation of economic power, and almost certainly of matching military power, is a great deal more certain than is the evolution of its political system in the direction of reliable internal checks and balances. The authority of the state to attempt to stop or curtail any aspect of its new openness to external influences remains absolute. And as long as other powers, particularly those proximate to China, have reservations about the reliability of the internal checks and balances on the freedom of China's leadership, they will incline toward stronger national means of resisting Chinese power; that is, they will feel compelled to 'hedge' against the image projected by China's leadership.

---

1 The administration of George W. Bush presided over a disturbingly severe erosion of US status in the world, and, for the first time, raised doubts about the capacity of America's internal checks and balances to reliably keep US power pointed in the 'right' direction. In response, a new cottage industry has sprung up in Washington policy circles devoted to 'doing by design' what the United States had for a century largely managed to do unconsciously. See, for example, Richard L. Armitage and Joseph S. Nye (co-Chairs), CSIS Commission on Smart Power: A Smarter, More Secure America, Center for Strategic & International Studies, Washington, DC, 2007, available at <http://www.csis.org/media/csis/pubs/071106_csissmartpowerreport.pdf>, accessed 24 June 2009.

China's system of governance also generates important tactical advantages in the 'game of nations' that Beijing exploits to the full. This has become particularly conspicuous in China's quest for resource and energy security. China has established itself most deeply with an array of states whose internal practices make them hazardous partners for the business community in the democratic world and which provide China with stronger opportunities to 'own' or 'control' their raw materials—states such as Myanmar, Zimbabwe, Nigeria and Sudan. On a positive note, however, it must be pointed out that the Chinese leadership also attaches genuine importance to perceptions of legitimacy regarding China's rise and, in respect of its dealings with Zimbabwe, Sudan, Myanmar (and, to a lesser extent, Iran), has demonstrated some sensitivity to its vulnerability in this regard.

A related observation is that China has no tradition of genuine partnership with another state. Moreover, it seems in no particular hurry to start such a tradition. For nearly all of its uniquely long history, China has been sufficiently large and powerful to essentially, in itself, define the 'system' for all the communities within its steadily expanding reach. It has, very occasionally, accepted other states as allies of convenience (the tribes of Inner Mongolia in the distant past, and both superpowers in the last century), but it has never formed a partnership with another significant state that it valued sufficiently to be prepared to be sensitive to and protective of the interests of the partner. Whether China can, or wants, to build such partnerships remains an open question.

Today's China, in my view, conveys the unmistakable impression of a state that is proceeding with great seriousness and determination to become a first-rank state with a balanced portfolio of power and no major vulnerabilities. China's leadership may not have a clear vision of what it would like to do when it achieves this status, nor of what international circumstances at that time will present in the way of opportunities and constraints. China's leadership does, however, seem to prefer postponing any discussions with its prospective peers on the modalities of their interaction until China is strong enough to have a decisive say on those modalities.

China takes itself very seriously and seems to be engaged in a quite stunning demonstration of Sun Tzu's dictum that 'to subdue the enemy without fighting is the supreme excellence', inviting the world to overlook the evidence about the formidable hard power assets it is determined to acquire in favour of simply enjoying the fruits of its market and trusting in the sincerity of its rhetoric on being determined to become a benign and peaceful new-age major power without a realist bone in its body.

One does not have to believe that China's rise is an ominous development to see prudence in questioning its endeavour to 'keep a low profile and hide its strengths' until some date in the still distant future. Playing along with this strategy, but also, inevitably, being driven to hedge against less optimistic scenarios, is a recipe for a steady erosion of trust and confidence, and the emergence of a serious adversarial relationship in circumstances of already heightened military preparedness. China is well past the point where any reasonable doubt can be attached either to its aspirations to become one of the world's dominant states or to its capacity to achieve these aspirations. It could be the case that the Chinese Government's rhetoric about the sort of international actor it intends to be is wholly sincere. It is the case, however, that China's system of governance inescapably erodes the credibility of that rhetoric. The policy prescription that emerges from this assessment is to become more persistent and resolute in requiring China to measure up to contemporary standards of openness and transparency, and to create opportunities for China to display its willingness to enter into obligations and commitments that genuinely constrain its policy options.

Bibliography

Armitage Richard L., and Joseph S. Nye (co-Chairs), CSIS Commission on Smart Power: A Smarter, More Secure America, Center for Strategic & International Studies, Washington, DC, 2007, available at <http://www.csis.org/media/csis/pubs/071106_csissmartpowerreport.pdf>, accessed 24 June 2009

Betts, Richard K., 'Wealth, Power and Instability: East Asia and the United States after the Cold War', International Security, vol. 18, no. 3, Winter 1993–94, pp. 34–77

Caldwell, Colonel John, China's Conventional Military Capabilities, 1994-2004: An Assessment, Center for Strategic and International Studies, Washington, DC, 1994

CIA World Factbook, available at <https://www.cia.gov/library/publications/the-world-factbook/rankorder/2004rank.html>, accessed 24 June 2009

Cliff, Roger, Mark Burles, Michael S. Chase, Derek Eaton, and Kevin L. Pollpeter, Entering the Dragon's Lair: Chinese Antiaccess Strategies and Their Implications for the United States, RAND Corporation, Santa Monica, 2007, available at <http://rand.org/pubs/monographs/MG524/>, accessed 24 June 2009

Clinton, Hillary Rodham, 'Clinton: Security and Opportunity for the Twenty-first Century', Foreign Affairs, vol. 86, no. 6, November/December 2007, pp. 2–18, available at <http://www.foreignaffairs.org/20071101faessay86601/hillary-rodham-clinton/security-and-opportunity-for-the-twenty-first-century.html>, accessed 24 June 2009

Clinton, William J., A National Security Strategy for a New Century, White House, Washington, DC, 1999, available at <http://www.au.af.mil/au/awc/awcgate/nss/nssr-1098.pdf>, accessed 24 June 2009

Cohen, Warren I., East Asia at the Center, Columbia University Press, New York, 2000

Cohen, William S., Report of the Quadrennial Defense Review, Washington, DC, May 1997

Council on Foreign Relations, Chinese Military Power, Report of an Independent Task Force, 2003, available at <http://www.cfr.org/content/publications/attachments/China_TF.pdf>, accessed 24 June 2009

Fairbank, John K. (ed.), The Chinese World Order: Traditional China's Foreign Relations, Harvard University Press, Cambridge, MA, 1968

Fairbank, John K., and Edwin O. Reischauer, China: Tradition and Transformation, Allen & Unwin, Sydney, 1989

Friedberg, Aaron L., 'Ripe for Rivalry: Prospects for Peace in a Multipolar World', International Security, vol. 18, no. 3, Winter 1993–94, pp. 5–33

Gaddis, John Lewis, We Now Know: Rethinking Cold War History, Oxford University Press, New York, 1997

Garver, John W., China and Iran: Ancient partners in a Post-Imperial World, University of Washington Press, Seattle, 2006

Gill, Bates, Rising Star: China's New Security Diplomacy, Brookings Institution Press, Washington, DC, 2007

Glasser, Bonnie S., 'Two Steps Forward, One Step Back', Comparative Connections, (An E-Journal on East Asian Bilateral Relations), 16 April 2002.

Glasser, Bonnie, Scott Snyder and John S. Park, 'Chinese Debate North Korea', PacNet Newsletter, 8 February 2008, available at <pacnet@hawaiibiz. rr.com>, accessed 20 June 2008

Goldstein, Avery, Rising to the Challenge: China's Grand Strategy and International Security, Stanford University Press, Stanford, 2005

Gungwu, Wang, 'Early Ming Relations With Southeast Asia: A Background Essay', in John K. Fairbank (ed.), The Chinese World Order: Traditional China's Foreign Relations, pp. 34–62

———, 'The Fourth Rise of China: Cultural Implications', China: An International Journal, vol. 2, September 2004, pp. 311–22

Hoagland, Jim, 'China: Two Enquires…', Washington Post, 20 July 1997

Huisken, Ron, 'Accelerating the Evolutionary Process of Security Cooperation in the Asia-Pacific: An Australian Perspective', in See Seng Tan and Amitav Acharya (eds), Asia-Pacific Security Cooperation: National Interests and Regional Order, M.E. Sharpe, Armonk, NY, 2004, pp. 38–42

———, America and China: A Long-Term Challenge for Statesmanship and Diplomacy, SDSC Working Paper no. 386, Strategic and Defence Studies Centre, The Australian National University, Canberra, March 2004

———, 'Iraq: The Neocon Strategy', Agenda, December 2006

————, QDR 2001: America's New Military Roadmap, SDSC Working Paper no. 366, Strategic and Defence Studies Centre, The Australian National University, Canberra, March 2002

International Institute for Strategic Studies, The Military Balance 2008, Routledge, London, February 2008

Kaplan, Robert D., 'How We Would Fight China', The Atlantic Monthly, June 2005, available at <http://www.theatlantic.com/doc/200506/kaplan>, accessed 24 June 2009

Kristensen, Hans M., Robert S. Norris and Matthew G. McKinzie, Chinese Nuclear Forces and US Nuclear War Planning, The Federation of American Scientists, and The Natural Resources Defense Council, November 2006, available at <http://www.nukestrat.com/china/chinareport.htm>, accessed 24 June 2009

Mann, James About Face: A History of America's Curious Relationship with China, from Nixon to Clinton, Alfred A. Knopf, New York, 1999

Marozzi, Justin, Tamerlane: Sword of Islam, Conqueror of the World, Da Capo Press, Cambridge, MA, 2006

Menzies, Gavin, 1421: The Year China Discovered America, Harper Collins Publishers, New York, 2003

Moore, Frank W., 'China's Military Capabilities', Institute for Defense & Disarmament Studies, Cambridge, MA, June 2000, available at <http://www.comw.org/cmp/fulltext/iddschina.html>, accessed 16 November 2009Office of the Secretary of Defense, Annual Report to the Congress, Military Power of the People's Republic of China, 2007, Washington, DC, 2007, available at <http://www.defenselink.mil/pubs/pdfs/070523-China-Military-Power-final.pdf>, accessed 24 June 2009

People's Republic of China, China's Endeavors for Arms Control, Disarmament and Non-Proliferation, White Paper, Beijing, September 2005. See 'Full text of White Paper on Arms Control', China Daily, available at <http://www.chinadaily.com.cn/english/doc/2005-09/01/content_474248.htm>, accessed 24 June 2009

Pillsbury Michael, (ed.), Chinese Views of Future Warfare, National Defense University Press, Washington, DC, 1997, available at <http://www.au.af.mil/au/awc/awcgate/ndu/chinview/chinacont.html>, accessed 24 June 2009

Pillsbury, Michael, 'PLA Capabilities in the 21st Century: How Does China Assess its Future Security Needs?', in Larry Wortzel (ed.), The Chinese

Armed Forces in the 21st Century, Strategic Studies Institute, US Army War College, Carlisle, PA, December 1999, pp. 89–158, available at <http://www.au.af.mil/au/awc/awcgate/ssi/chin21cent.pdf>, accessed 16 November 2009

Pomfret, John, 'In Fact and in Tone, US Expresses New Fondness for Taiwan', Washington Post, 30 April 2002

Richelson, Jeffrey T., Spying on the Bomb: American Nuclear Intelligence from Nazi Germany to Iran and North Korea, W.W. Norton & Company, New York, 2006

Rumsfeld, Donald H., Secretary of Defense, Quadrennial Defense Review Report, Washington, DC, 30 September 2001

———, Secretary of Defense, Quadrennial Defense Review Report, Washington, DC, 6 February 2006, available at <http://www.defenselink.mil/qdr/report/Report20060203.pdf>, accessed 24 June 2009

Schwartz, Benjamin I., 'The Chinese Perception of World Order, Past and Present', in John K. Fairbank, (ed.), The Chinese World Order: Traditional China's Foreign Relations, Harvard University Press, Cambridge, 1968, pp. 276–291

Sheridan, Michael, 'China plotted Hong Kong invasion', Australian, 25 June 2007

Sperling, Eliot, The Tibet-China Conflict: History and Polemics, Policy Studies, no. 7, East-West Center, Washington, DC, 2004, available at <http://www.eastwestcenter.org/fileadmin/stored/pdfs/PS007.pdf>, accessed 24 June 2009

Stockholm International Peace Research Institute, SIPRI Yearbook 2006, Oxford University Press, Oxford, 2006

Sutter, Robert G., China's Rise in Asia, Rowman & Littlefield, Lanham, MD, 2005

Suyin, Han, Eldest Son: Zhou Enlai and the Making of Modern China 1989-1976, Kodansha, New York, 1994

Swaine, Michael D., and Ashley J. Tellis, Interpreting China's Grand Strategy: Past, Present, and Future, Rand Corporation, Santa Monica, 2000, available at <http://rand.org/pubs/monograph_reports/MR1121/>, accessed 24 June 2009

Swaine, Michael D., Zhang Tuosheng and Danielle F.S. Cohen (eds), Managing Sino-American Crises: Case Studies and Analysis, Carnegie Endowment for International Peace, Washington, DC, 2000

Terrill, Ross, The New Chinese Empire and What It Means for the United States, Basic Books, New York, 2004

Thayer, Carlyle A., 'China's International Security Cooperation with Southeast Asia', Australian Defence Force Journal, no. 172, 2007

van Marrewijk, Charles, International Trade and the World Economy, Oxford University Press, Oxford, February 2002

Wall, Robert, 'China Defense Budget Could Double by 2005', Aviation Week & Space Technology, 25 March 2002, p. 33.

Wilson, Andrew R., 'War and the East', address to the Foreign Policy Research Institute's History Institute for Teachers conference on 'Teaching Military History: Why and How', 29–30 September 2007, available at <http://www.fpri.org/education/teachingmilitaryhistory/>, accessed 24 June 2009World Military Expenditure and Arms Transfers, US Arms Control and Disarmament Agency, Washington, DC

Wortzel, Larry M. China's Nuclear Forces: Operations, Training, Doctrine, Command, Control, and Campaign Planning, Strategic Studies Institute, US Army War College, Carlisle, PA, May 2007, available at <http://www.strategicstudiesinstitute.army.mil/pdffiles/PUB776.pdf>, accessed 16 April 2008

Xiaoping, Deng, 'Speech to an Enlarged Meeting of the Military Commission of the Party Central Committee' (14 July 1975), Selected Works of Deng Xiaoping, Beijing, 1 July 1983, in Joint Publications Research Service, China Report, Foreign Broadcast Information Service, Reston, VA, 31 October 1983, p. 19

Zoellick, Robert B., US Deputy Secretary of State, 'Whither China: From Membership to Responsibility?', National Committee on US-China Relations, 21 September 2005

www.ingramcontent.com/pod-product-compliance
Lightning Source LLC
Chambersburg PA
CBHW061241270326
41927CB00035B/3465